797.1
A

Anderson

A guide t

797.1
A

Anderson

A guide to canoe camping

A Guide to Canoe Camping

A Guide
to Canoe
Camping

by Luther A. Anderson

Illustrated By Richard Lowe

797.1
AND

REILLY & LEE · *Chicago*

797.1
A

Foreword

Canoeing as a form of outdoor enjoyment stands to-day on the threshold of immense popularity. It is an excellent form of recreation for outdoorsmen, young people at summer camp, and, equally, a family or an individual. In each of the fifty states, as well as in Canada, there are canoeing waters—lakes, rivers, streams—many of them spreading through country rich in wildlife and of breathtaking natural beauty. There are waters to suit every taste, from the still, moss-shrouded waters of a Florida swamp to the clear streams of the West, and from the fast waters of the Ozarks to the myriad remote lakes of the northern states. For every canoe enthusiast, whether city- or country-dweller, there is a stream or lake accessible for weekend recreation, and there can be as much enjoyment in the short trip down a local stream as there is in the long cruise into backwoods country.

In many cities there are clubs that sponsor weekend canoeing, and this sort of activity is growing in popularity. (For example, there are the YMCA, the AYH, and the Boy and Girl Scouts of America as well as local canoeing associations.) These organizations realize what potential this type of outdoor activity has in developing mind and body, and they promote it to a fine degree on lakes and streams throughout the country.

The canoe-camping trip at once combines the exercise of skills with recreation, relaxation, and the discovery of the countryside. Moreover, the canoe cruise is just what the canoeist makes of it. It is no longer only for people who have their own canoeing equipment. In many places there are canoe rentals available to assist the weekend canoeist and his family in planning for a few hours' or a few days' pleasure in a canoe. Along many major canoe waters there are canoe liveries and outfitters who will furnish whatever the canoeist needs. They can make a one- or two-week canoe trip a pleasure, at minimal expense to the canoe camper. Their services include furnishing lightweight modern canoes, camping and sleeping equipment, and food supplies. Or the canoeist may rent only the canoe, if he wishes, and take care of the rest of the outfit himself.

These outfitters are experienced, helpful woodsmen, and they will be glad to mark on large-scale maps the points of interest, the better campsites, and the best fishing areas on the route. They can also recommend a guide service if one is needed.

Whether the canoe cruise is short or long, a leisurely family jaunt or a trip into the wilderness to test self-reliance and resourcefulness, it will let you into the thrill and satisfaction of this sport of primitive skills.

This book will discuss the questions concerning the longer, more involved, and more demanding kinds of canoe cruising, the canoe trip into the wilds. But in so doing, it will cover information pertinent to all types of canoe camping; for the principles of canoeing and camping apply in some measure to all canoe cruises, whether long or short, on rough water or calm lake, with copious or minimal equipment. And consequently this is a book for beginner and expert alike.

The author has drawn on the experiences of many canoe campers in preparing this book, and he would like to thank many more than he can mention. In particular, however, he would like to single out Art Mercier, of C.B.S. radio in Chicago; Walter M. Kiplinger, Jr., and Barry S. Tindall, of the National Recreation and Park Association; the Coleman Company, Inc., of Wichita, Kansas; Jim Pascoe, of Wilderness Outfitters, Inc.; and Ralph Frese, of the Chicagoland Canoe Base. To all of these, and especially to the latter, go the author's grateful thanks for their comments and suggestions.

Luther A. Anderson

Contents

1

Getting Organized

Sometime—maybe early in the spring—it's bound to happen. A companion makes a chance remark, or you're poring over an old map, or you recall a conversation about some remote place or beautiful stretch of country. Suddenly you feel a strange restlessness to be out and away, a yearning for a far-off region, or for a weekend or more spent in complete relaxation and peace on a nearby lake.

Then it is time to get your gear in shape to confront nature in her many moods—and of course you must make the journey by canoe, the way of the Indian, the *voyageur,* and the early American explorer in years long past.

For many outdoorsmen, canoe travel is the true way to find their special brand of happiness, to test their pluck and skill and ingenuity. For such men, when the restlessness hits them, there is nothing to do but to summon fellow enthusiasts and begin making plans for a canoe trip.

Your Companions

It is most important to remember that different people are suited to different kinds of canoe trips. Everyone can enjoy a one- or two-day trip on a lake or river, but not everyone will want to set off on a one- or two-week expedition into the wilds. The canoe party must decide on the kind of trip it wants—a short excursion of a couple of days into a resort region, a long vacation into the wilds, or some combination of the two.

More than one canoeist has ruined the outing for a whole party because his idea of a good time did not coincide with that of the others. Some canoe travelers like to head for a lake and camp for the rest of the time. Others want to set a distant goal and travel all the time, over a rough route with many portages. Still others take a canoe trip simply to enjoy the scenery and to discover and explore a certain area.

Talk it over with the others of the crew. Find out what each wishes to do so that there will be no disagreement later as to destination and the way the trip should be run. Living in the woods for a week or two may very definitely not be some people's idea of enjoyment, and the time to find out is before the trip begins, not after it has started.

One man should be the party's leader, and this should be the man with the most experience in canoe camping, one who has proved himself in the outdoors. When there are decisions to make, this is the man who should make them. Chances are that he will organize the trip in the first place, select equipment, food supplies, and the way the trip should be run, and this individual should always have the cooperation of the other campers. If he doesn't, he won't be a very effective leader, and the trip could end in confusion, ill-feelings, and even disaster.

If you are the leader and are planning a long trip, short jaunts on weekends with prospective partners will soon disclose their tempers, likes and dislikes, and general reactions to life in the woods, and you will be able to judge whether they are willing to endure discomforts and have a love of adventure and feeling for the outdoors—all of which are necessary for the successful long canoe trip.

In this way you will make sure that your companions have both the necessary skill and the ability to get along with one another. Of course, on shorter trips you need be less careful in making your selection, but skill and compatibility are qualities you can never fully neglect.

Once the canoe party has been organized, find out at the outset what your trip will cost and what each man can afford, and then keep within the budget. The expenses are usually shared, and careful planning to ensure that the proper supplies are taken is essential. What supplies you take, however, will depend very much on the route you choose.

The Route

Selecting the route is always very important. All your planning decisions must be geared to the route you plan to take. If the territory is unfamiliar, you will want detailed maps describing the topography of the region and what conditions to expect for canoe travel. The United States Department of the Interior provides detailed maps of most areas of the country. These maps cost little and are one of the best sources of information available for planning a trip and learning about the area you plan to visit.

If you are planning a canoe trip to a remote area, it is advisable to contact someone who has been there before you. If the trip is not too far distant from habitation, a letter to the chamber of commerce in a nearby town will usually bring you valuable information about the area.

Conservation agencies in any state you wish to visit are good sources of information, too. These agencies issue booklets and maps on the canoe trails, campsites, and other features of their states. (A list of agencies and their addresses in the United States and Canada can be found in Chapter 19 and in Appendix I.)

The right contact will provide maps showing the length of possible trips, campsites along the way, rapids, portages, trails, towns, etc., and will furnish you with a list of guides available.

Some of the most popular canoe trips start

along the United States-Canadian border. A canoe trip through the Quetico-Superior National-Provincial Park, for example, is a passport to some really breathtaking country. It brings the canoeist to landlocked lakes where motorboats are unknown, into wild country of awesome beauty, to magnificent waterfalls, to fishing spots out of this world, and to glimpses of animals in their native habitat.

At convenient places in this and other canoe areas, there are outfitters well equipped to supply not only the food for the outing but canoes and gear as well, and to advise any prospective canoe traveler about routes. The service is generally professional and reliable. These men have been over the routes and can anticipate the needs of the canoe party. For example, in and around Ely and Grand Marais, Minnesota, and Oxtongue Lake and Sioux Lookout, Ontario, canoe outfitters will furnish you with canoes and gear and accurate maps of the region, inform you of the best camping sites along the way, furnish food supplies, and advise you how to make the trip really enjoyable, warning you, for example, of local hazards, pests, new natural and artificial obstacles, and weather expectations, so that the cruise will be a pleasure jaunt and not a grueling grind. If you want the latter, you can always have it. But most people are willing to foot the modest bill for the usually excellent advice, information, and supplies the outfitters provide.

The Supplies

More will be said on supplies in Chapters 12 and 16, but it is well to remember one rule: travel light, but without reducing yourself to a spartan existence. Keep your duffel bags well packed, but with an eye only for the necessary items. For example, you may wish to take along a portable stove. It takes some room, but it is very welcome, especially on wet days. Likewise, though tent pegs can be cut, there are light aluminum pegs on the market that weigh little and serve nicely.

Little by little you will find yourself gaining independence, self-reliance, and resourcefulness. Thus, you may eventually decide to leave behind that stove when you find that it is great fun to cut your own fuel, where available, and do your cooking over the campfire.

The canoeist is on his own for the most part. He must meet many a problem thrown into his path by the exigencies of the moment. If he is outfitted properly and has a basic understanding of woodcraft, canoemanship, and navigation, he should be able to enjoy his trip to the utmost, whether the weather be rough and stormy or sunny and bright.

2

The
Canoe

More than three hundred years ago Samuel de Champlain, the great explorer, told his superiors that the only way to get around in America was by means of the Indian birchbark canoe, a craft the first Spanish explorers had found the Indians using.

Thus the canoe is an old and versatile friend. Long before it was thought of as a recreational craft, it provided a way into the wilderness for explorers and trappers, and it played a vital role in the commercial life of early America. For centuries before the arrival of the first Europeans, indeed, it provided a means of travel, of transporting food and goods, and of communicating between settlements and tribes. Thus, over many generations, the canoe has been important to many peoples, a very practical and necessary part of life.

A craft that survives the progress of so many centuries must be adaptable and handy. But basic canoe design has changed little. A canoe is still long and narrow and pointed at both ends, still designed for speed and portability, and still propelled over deep and shallow water by means of paddles or poles. And it remains the best way of traveling the lakes, ponds, streams, and rivers that are the water-wilderness of North America.

There are several types of canoe. The Eskimo kayak, the dugout, and the pirogue of Louisiana are all canoes, but *the* canoe is the traditional birchbark Indian canoe and its descendants. The Indian canoe has changed substantially only in materials. Thus, in the 1870's the first wooden canoe was built, in Canada, and in the 1890's the canvas canoe with a wooden frame first made its appearance. Canoes are still made of wood or of wood and canvas today, but much more popular are aluminum and fiber-glass canoes.

Canoe Terminology

For the sake of easy reference, you should be familiar with a certain amount of canoe terminology, a partial list of which follows.

Ahead – in front of the canoe
Astern – behind the canoe
Amidships – the middle of the canoe
Bow – the forward section of the canoe
Stern – the rear section of the canoe
Forward – toward the bow
Aft – toward the stern
Bowman – the front, or bow, paddler
Sternman – the rear, or stern, paddler
Windward – the side from which the wind blows
Leeward – the downwind side of the canoe
Port – the left side of the canoe, facing forward
Starboard – the right side of the canoe, facing forward
Freeboard – the distance from the waterline to the gunwale, amidships
L.O.A. – the complete length, "length over all," of the canoe, from tip to tip

Some important terms need more explanation. The *beam* of the canoe is the hull's transverse measurement at its widest part, amidships. Since width will affect stability, because it dictates the amount of the hull in contact with the water, the general rule is that the wider the beam, the more stable the canoe. The *depth* of the canoe is the perpendicular measurement from the middle of the bottom of the hull, inside the canoe, to a point midway between, and level with the top of, the gunwales at the beam. The most usual depth is 12 inches. The *tumble home* is the curvature of the side of the canoe between waterline and gunwale. A canoe with a wide tumble home (sides with a pronounced curve) will tend to ship water in rough conditions more easily than one with a narrow tumble home.

Canoe Parts

There are three popular kinds of canoe—wood-and-canvas, aluminum, and fiber-glass. They differ mainly in their materials, but also in some details of construction. In identifying parts of the canoe, remember that, though not all canoes are built the same way, most do have certain standard parts. Using the wood-and-canvas canoe as an example, we can identify the standard parts found on almost every canoe. (Figure 1)

Gunwales (pronounced "gunnels"). The gunwales are comprised of two strips, an inside strip, the inwale, and an outside strip, the outwale, that run around the upper edge of the canoe and function as a rim. In wood-and-canvas canoes the inwale is made of spruce and the outwale of hardwood.

Decks. The decks are the small triangular blocks at the bow and stern of the canoe filling the space between the gunwales. In wood-and-canvas canoes they are usually made of straight-grained hardwood; in fiber-glass canoes they are usually molded in.

Ribs. The ribs hold the canoe together in a transverse framework. They give the canoe its distinctive shape. In wood-and-canvas canoes they are made of white cedar.

Thwarts. The thwarts are the transverse braces that hold the gunwales apart. In the larger canoes there is a bow, center, and stern thwart. In the wood-

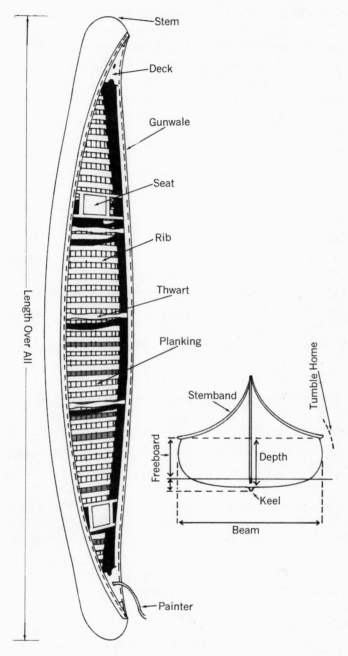

Labels on figure:
Stem
Deck
Gunwale
Seat
Rib
Thwart
Planking
Length Over All
Stemband
Tumble Home
Freeboard
Depth
Keel
Beam
Painter

Figure 1
The Canoe and Its Parts

and-canvas canoe they are made of wood; in the aluminum, of aluminum tubing; and in the fiber-glass canoe of molded fiber glass, aluminum, or wood. Indeed, some fiber-glass canoes have gunwales, seats, and thwarts molded in one piece and fastened to the hull.

Seats. There are usually two seats, one just in front of the stern thwart and the other just behind the bow thwart. For paddling comfort, they should be a few inches below, but fastened to, the gunwales. Seats may be dispensed with in favor of "paddling thwarts," thwarts that serve also as seats. In fiber-glass canoes the seats are often molded to the gunwales, thereby contributing to the sturdiness of the canoe.

Painters. Painters are lines fixed to bow and stern by means of small holes drilled through the decks. Each line should be at least half the L.O.A. Painters are used for tying up the canoe for short periods and for towing.

Keels. The keel is a strip of wood, aluminum, or fiber glass that is attached to the center of the underside of the canoe and runs from bow to stern.

There are two keel styles, the *lake keel* and the *shoe keel,* and some canoes have no keel at all. The lake keel is about one inch square and is designed to prevent sideslipping in wind and open water. The shoe keel is twice as wide and half as thick as the lake keel and is useful in protecting the bottom of the canoe from rocks, logs, sandbars, and the like, and it also permits easy navigation and turning in the rapids. The shoe keel is considered best for all around use. A keel of some sort is desirable in all canoes, since it adds stability to the canoe as a whole. On the other hand, however, canoes without keels enjoy maximum maneuverability.

The wood-and-canvas canoe has some additional features worth mentioning, especially since some are shared by other types of canoes. First, it has a *stem,* a curved piece of hardwood at each end of the canoe to which planking, decks, and ribs are attached. All wood-and-canvas canoes have inside stems, and some also have outside stems. The stems are often protected against jars and abrasions by brass or aluminum *stembands*.

The aluminum canoe also has stems, pieces of aluminum to which the hull's sidesheets are riveted.

Wood-and-canvas canoes have *planking*. Usually made of red cedar 5/32 inch thick and 4 inches wide, the planking runs the length of the canoe. To it are fastened the ribs and stems.

3

Choosing a Canoe

Canoes vary in many ways: materials used in construction, length, depth, purpose, etc. And to assess the value of a canoe properly, it is necessary to be familiar with all such differences.

Types of Canoes

The Wood-and-Canvas Canoe. The wood-and-canvas canoe is still being made and is a superb performer, but it is rather fragile and requires regular treatment with paint and varnish and more maintenance than the aluminum or fiber-glass craft. Then, too, the hull will absorb moisture when continuously in the water, and over a summer this weight can amount to as much as 12 pounds. In addition to being the traditional canoe, however, the wood-and-canvas canoe is also approximately 10 per cent faster than the aluminum model, is the easiest hull to paddle, and is preferred by fishermen and hunters because it is the quietest canoe. Finally it is by far the most aesthetically pleasing model.

Modern technology, moreover, has made it possible to eliminate the moisture-absorbing factor in wood-and-canvas canoes by replacing the canvas cover with fiber glass, as in the Old Town "Trapper" canoe, for example.

The Aluminum Canoe. A canoe of great popularity is the aluminum. It is light (varying with the model), sturdy, reliable, and inexpensive, and it requires a minimum of care.

The aluminum canoe's factory finish is harsh-looking, with an objectionable shine. But give it a coat of paint, and the aluminum canoe takes on a more pleasing appearance; or leave it unpainted, and the metal assumes a weathered patina that is pleasing to the eye, though it will oxidize and rub off on clothing and gear.

The aluminum canoe has other disadvantages, too. It is the most difficult to repair on a trip, requiring rivets and sealing compound. It absorbs heat, making canoeing uncomfortable on torrid days or in the sun, and in cold weather it is cold. It is also very noisy: when running shallow streams, it sounds like a garbage can rolling down the street in a high wind.

However, aluminum is highly favored by many sportsmen, camps, and rental liveries because it needs so little maintenance, and it is safe, for almost all aluminum canoes have foam flotation chambers.

The Fiber-Glass Canoe. The fiber-glass canoe is light and very strong, trim, and durable, and it currently enjoys great favor. This canoe has a permanent color and requires minimal painting and maintenance. It is the easiest canoe to repair; fiber-glass repair kits are small, easy to use, and inexpensive.

Fiber glass lends itself to the construction of fine hulls, and fiber-glass canoes are quieter than aluminum canoes, though less quiet than wood-and-canvas canoes.

An additional feature of fiber-glass canoes, of interest to canoeing families in particular, is the non-skid surface.

Magnesium, Royalite, Cycolac Canoes. Magnesium canoes are still to be found but are no longer being built. They are extremely light, but the metal has a tendency to fatigue and collapse. Royalite canoes are made from an expanded rubber material. They have not enjoyed much success and should be avoided.

Cycolac canoes, made with a new thermal plastic with great impact resistance, are still in the experimental state. It seems quite possible, however, that cycolac will provide a viable alternative in canoe construction.

The Birchbark Canoe. These canoes are still made, but they are very expensive and not very practical.

From an aesthetic standpoint the cedar-and-canvas canoe is by far the most beautiful. But it requires constant attention to keep it in top shape and needs to be treated and handled like fine old furniture. For practical reasons, aluminum canoes are the most popular, with fiber-glass canoes second.

General Rules

Select the canoe that best fits your requirements. Do you want it for a day's canoeing or a week's canoeing? For canoeing in local waters, white-water canoeing in rock-strewn rivers, or canoe-camping trips? For racing or wilderness travel? For some combination of these activities? You will have to make the choice. If you are going to use a canoe in white water, don't get a wood-and-canvas model; it is too easily seriously damaged. If you are going to have to portage often, get a lightweight canoe that is strongly constructed; for example, a softwood-and-canvas model with hardwood gunwales, thwarts, and decks, or a lightweight aluminum canoe.

Remember, too, to take into account such factors as the length of the trip and the size of the party. All these considerations—weight, length, water, size of party, number of portages to be made—will affect your choice. Consequently, one can only learn *general rules*, which each prospective canoe purchaser should use as guide lines:

1. The larger and wider the canoe, the greater the weight and carrying capacity.

2. The narrower the canoe, the greater the ease in getting through water and the more advantage you can

take of the canoe's momentum.

3. The wider the canoe, the greater the stability. Consequently, it is a fact that a wide, flat-bottomed canoe has the greatest stability *in ideal conditions.* In fact, the farther forward and aft the full width is taken, the more stable the canoe will be. But this canoe will be relatively slow and will make for hard work. In addition, in any rough water it will have a tendency to "bob" and "pound." A narrow canoe with a sharply curved bottom will lack stability and maneuverability, and it will tend to cut into waves, instead of lifting over them, and, as a result, ship water in rough conditions. The best canoe, therefore, is neither too narrow nor too wide. Such a canoe will be maneuverable, especially with the addition of a keel, while remaining quite stable. In rough water it will not bob, nor will it knife dangerously through waters; it will ride over them.

4. A canoe with a slight curve to its bottom will be more maneuverable than one with a straight bottom line (because it will have a better-defined axis), and it will tend to rise and fall with the waves.

5. The greater the depth and the higher the ends, the more the canoe will be affected by winds, especially crosswinds, but the less water it will ship, especially if it has a narrow tumble home. Remember, however, that canoe depth should vary, depending on the kind of water and load expected. In quiet waters the depth need not be great (about 11 inches); for river water the canoe should be a little deeper; for lakes a little deeper still; and for long trips with a heavy load, a deep canoe is definitely indicated. Appropriate canoe depth is less for smooth-water travel and greater for rough-water travel. The best compromise is an average depth (12 inches) with slightly raised ends (to deal with waves).

6. A keel adds stability but diminishes maneuverability. A canoe with a keel is less likely to be blown off course by the wind or to swing from side to side in

response to strokes, and the keel provides protection for the canoe bottom, which is very important. A shoe keel is probably the best compromise.

7. A wide outwale will give strength to the canoe and help turn back wave splash, thereby lessening the need for excessive depth, especially if there is a narrow tumble home. A narrow inwale will make easier the task of emptying a swamped or partially waterlogged canoe.

8. Higher seats will make paddling easier because paddling will require less "stretch" and effort. But they will increase instability by fixing the center of gravity higher in the canoe. Some little stability, however, should be sacrificed for the increase in paddling comfort.

To sum up: probably the best all-around canoe is relatively narrow, has a slightly rounded hull that is curved longitudinally, fine hull lines, slightly upturned ends, a shoe keel, a wide outwale, a narrow inwale, and seats set only an inch or so below the gunwale.

Length Over All

If the canoe is going to be used largely for solo paddling, or equally for solo and tandem paddling, the 16-foot canoe is probably the best. If, however, it is likely to be used mostly for tandem paddling, a 17-foot canoe would prove most useful. The 16-foot and 17-foot canoes are the most popular, but for extended trips and large parties an 18-foot canoe might be advisable. It is well to remember that a long canoe is faster, even if there is only one paddler, than a short canoe, because it generates more momentum, and no canoeist should be put off by the thought that he would tire with a long canoe.

On the other hand, of course, large canoes are heavier—a factor to be taken into account if the canoe is for a youngster (a 15-foot canoe is probably best for him), or if there is much portaging to do.

For a party of three making an extended lake-and-river trip, the 18-footer is the best choice. Such a canoe will carry up to two months' provisions for three men and the camp outfit. For three men, a smaller model would require too much exertion to be moved through the water in heavy winds, because the canoe would ride too low in the water. It would certainly not be as safe as a larger canoe. A larger canoe has a greater capacity, and it will therefore ride higher in the water than a smaller canoe with the same load, giving more freeboard, and will take less effort for the paddlers to push it through the water.

Flotation

One very important consideration in choosing a canoe is the matter of flotation. When wood-and-canvas canoes were used exclusively, there was no need for flotation chambers because wood is a naturally buoyant material, and wooden canoes will float when capsized. Aluminum and fiber-glass canoes, however, are not self-buoyant and need flotation chambers for safety.

At one time, both air pockets and foam-filled chambers were used for flotation, but air pockets have been discontinued because their value is destroyed by puncture and because leaks can develop without the canoeist's being aware of them. Now most aluminum and fiber-glass canoes have flotation chambers that are filled with a spongy, lightweight plastic material full of closed cells, such as polyurethane foam, built into the covered portion of bow and stern, and sometimes also under the gunwales.

Conclusion

If you are at all unsure about which model to choose, seek expert advice and insist on a canoe made by a reliable company. Poorly made and ill-handling canoes are bad buys. The canoeist who selects the best craft, even though it is higher priced than another model, will be ahead in the long run.

4

Canoe Accessories

As important as a good canoe are good accessories, particularly paddles. Unless you equip yourself with the proper paddles, you will find that the money you spent on getting the canoe of your choice will be largely wasted, as will also be much of the energy you expended moving it through the water.

Paddles

The *paddle* is the most important canoe accessory, and the most commonly used is the single-blade model.

It is the rule of thumb that the bowman's paddle length should be such that when the paddle is resting on the ground and the canoeist is standing straight, it reaches his chin, and the sternman's his eye. The average paddle is therefore 57–66 inches long. The chin- and eye-level measurements are traditional, but you may find another length that suits you better. The ultimate goals in selecting a paddle length are efficiency in moving the canoe and comfort to the paddler. In fact, many canoeists tend to use a slightly longer paddle, especially if the paddle is light and paddling is done from the seat instead of from a kneeling position. The average *blade* is 6½ inches wide and 27 inches long.

Weight is the most important feature in a paddle, for it will be handled times without number in the course of a day. Consequently, it is best to get a light, softwood paddle. Those made of three or five pieces, though more expensive, are better than those made of one piece of wood, because paddles of the latter construction split and break more easily. All paddles should be examined carefully for knots, and the canoeist should make sure that the grain in the shaft is straight.

Average softwood paddle weight is 1¾ pounds, but a lighter paddle can be used—provided great care is taken to prevent its damage. Generally speaking, and especially in rougher water, the regulation paddle is indicated, but a heavier paddle also should be taken along for use in shallow or rocky waters and to act as a spare in case of damage or loss to the other.

Another very important characteristic of a good paddle is *flexibility*. A flexible paddle will yield to the water and provide more power than a rigid one, and the canoeist will appreciate this quality at the end of a day of paddling.

While you can fashion a paddle yourself from a length of cedar or other kind of tree, it is best and easiest to take care of the one you have. If you are on a trip with a number of other people and you've brought along your favorite paddle, you might want to mark it with colored tape or some other device to identify it as yours.

There are several styles and types of paddles. Two of these, as well as the parts of a paddle, are shown in Figure 2.

Softwood Paddles. The softwood paddle, usually made of spruce, is light, strong, and fine for most canoe travel; it will stand a good deal of pressure. Since it is made of soft wood, though, the blade must be used with care and kept from sharp contact with rocks, stumps, deadheads, sandbars, and the like. (This is even more important if you use an ultra-light paddle, such as one made of cedar.) Rough use may result in splitting and certainly in brooming (the fraying and flattening of the end of the paddle caused by

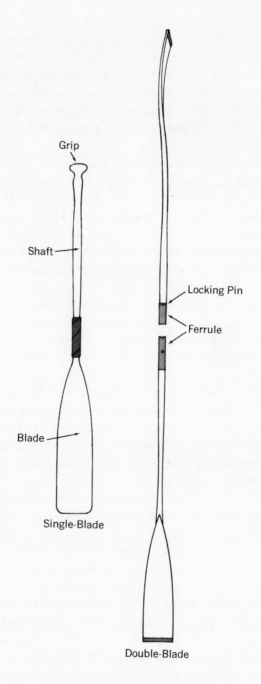

Figure 2
Paddles and Their Parts

stubbing it on hard surfaces). These defects should be repaired on the spot.

Hardwood Paddles. Hardwood paddles are usually made from ash or maple, and although heavier than a spruce paddle of equal size, they can be considerably lightened by thinning. The average hardwood paddle will take a lot of punishment without splitting or breaking. It is often taken along as an auxiliary, for it does provide a certain change of pace after long use of the spruce paddle and is very valuable in shallow and rocky water, where softwood paddles could easily be damaged.

Laminated Paddles. Laminated paddles made of many thin layers of wood glued together are becoming popular. A good laminated paddle will provide great strength at no increase in weight, but care should be taken to purchase a quality product, which is often difficult to obtain. The glues in cheaper laminated paddles sometimes dissolve after prolonged immersion.

Double-Blade Paddles. A paddle useful at times, especially on a solo cruise, is the double-blade paddle, which is comparable to, though longer than, the paddle used by Eskimos in kayaks. These paddles permit quick and strong paddling and a fast pickup, and they are therefore very useful in strong winds.

The best double-blade paddles are made of spruce, and when fitted with copper tips, they will stand up admirably under normal and rough water conditions. The best length for the double-blade when used with a standard 15- to 18-foot canoe is 9–10 feet. The blades should be set at right angles to each other, to allow for "feathering" the blade in the wind: the blade in the air will have its edge and not its full surface exposed to the wind and will therefore offer less resistance to forward motion. Double-blade paddles are sometimes made with blades at right angles to each other, but often the desired angle can be obtained simply by adjusting the locking metal ferrule in the center of the paddle. (This locking ferrule also allows you to set the blades horizontally, to take advantage of a strong following wind.) If the paddle blades are horizontal and cannot be adjusted, a feathering effect can be obtained by slightly twisting the left or right hand, to present the blade in the air at an angle to the wind.

The double-blade paddle serves well as an extra paddle, too, and it is extremely useful in the family canoe when one parent is left to do all the paddling while the other looks after the young children.

Kneeling Pads

Traditionally, the canoeist kneels in his canoe, and many still choose this method. For maximum efficiency, in white water, for example, the kneeling position cannot be improved upon.

However, kneeling, to those not used to it, is uncomfortable, unless some padding is used. Cheap, effective pads can easily be made of old hot-water bottles, inner tubing, sponge rubber, and even a temporarily discarded tennis shoe. A most useful dual purpose pad is a large *sponge*, for it also makes the most effective bailing device.

A canoe can also be rigged for rowing and sailing, but since these modifications are somewhat specialized, they will not be dealt with in this book.

5

Getting Afloat

Much damage is done to the canoe before it ever gets to the water. It is therefore essential to know how to treat the canoe when carrying, launching, loading, boarding, and landing it.

Carrying the Canoe by Car

Most canoes are transported over land by car; consequently a car rack is very useful. But with or without a rack, the canoe should be thickly padded where it touches metal, for the good of both the car and the canoe. *The canoe must be tied down firmly front and back and on the sides.* More damage is sustained by a canoe in transit than at any other time, so stop from time to time when carrying the canoe and test the lashings. The more you transport a canoe, the more you appreciate a car rack that accommodates a canoe tightly and well.

If you belong to a club or have more than one canoe yourself, you will probably find a canoe trailer, which can carry several canoes, useful.

Carrying the Canoe Short Distances

When you want to lift the canoe from the car top or rack and there is no one to help you, stand beside the car facing forward, rest the back of your right arm against the car, and lever the canoe toward you. Then grasp the gunwale nearer you with your left hand, reach under the canoe with your right hand, and pull the canoe up and toward you until it is balancing on the gunwale that was farther from you. Make sure you are standing amidships, balance the canoe with your left hand, lock your right elbow against your side, and with your right hand lift the canoe off and carry it to the water's edge.

At the water's edge, lower the canoe by first letting your right hand slip around the hull, so that the canoe slides into the crook of your arm, and then swinging the canoe around and down so that it is resting on your thighs. Then, grasping the nearer gunwale amidships with both hands, lower the canoe to the ground. As you do so, let the canoe roll over so that it is in an upright position.

For moving a canoe very short distances, grasp a gunwale amidships with both hands and lift the canoe to your hip. (Figure 3)

This also is the way to begin to lift the canoe to your shoulder. Lift the canoe amidships with both

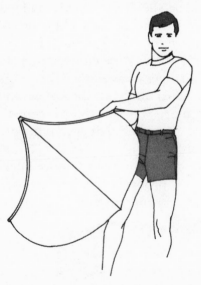

Figure 3
One-Man Carry, Short Distance (I)

Figure 4
One-Man Carry, Short Distance (II)

hands, stoop, and rest the canoe on your thighs. Press down on the gunwale nearer you and grasp the far gunwale with your left hand. The canoe should now be balancing on your thighs on the gunwale that was nearer you. Slip your right hand under the canoe so that your right elbow cradles the gunwale and then, with a boost from your knee if necessary, straighten up and swing the canoe up and through 45 degrees. Finally, adjust your right hand so that it is under the gunwale; your left hand will be overhead, grasping the upper gunwale and balancing the canoe. (Figure 4)

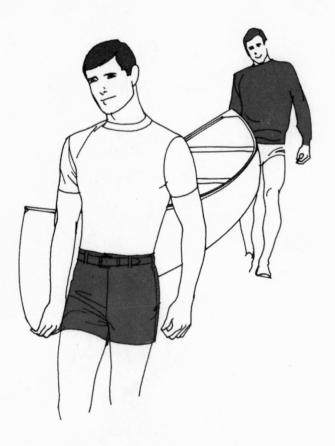

Figure 5
Two-Man Carry, Short Distance

When there are two persons to carry the canoe, they should take hold of the ends and carry the canoe bottom down. Both canoeists should be on the same side and use the same arm. The front man should, however, invert his arm to counteract any tendency the canoe may have to tip over. (Figure 5)

These methods of carrying a canoe will be found to work for short distances, but other methods are useful when distance is involved. Portaging, however, is covered in Chapter 9.

Figure 6
Two-Man Launch, at Dock

Getting the Canoe into and out of the Water

Where there is a dock, launch the canoe parallel to this projection. If there are two persons, each should hold an end; if there is one person, he should lift the canoe amidships and place it in the water. (Figure 6)

If possible, even when there is no dock, the canoe should be launched parallel to the shore. But sometimes this is impossible (where it is very marshy, where there is a very small landing area or many rocks,

Figure 7
One-Man Launch, End-On

etc.). Then it should be launched bow first. If two people are launching the canoe, they should each hold a gunwale amidships and then, hand over hand, launch the canoe into the water. If there is only one person, he should lift the canoe onto his thighs and then slide it over his thighs into the water. (Figure 7)

To get the canoe out of the water, reverse the process.

Boarding the Canoe

Most damage to a canoe is done while it is on land. On land it is a solid object that can be easily damaged, but in the water it is a buoyant and responsive thing. But damage can still occur unless the canoe is *floating freely* before *any* weight is added to it. Never board the canoe while even one end is up on shore. Never load it on shore. Likewise, before beaching the canoe on shore preparatory to portaging, empty it.

When the canoe can be brought parallel to a dock or the shore, one man steadies it while the other boards. Board it by stepping firmly into it *over the keel line*. It is not necessary to step into the canoe amidships *provided* that you step into the canoe over the keel line. (Figure 8) When the first man (the stern-man usually) is in, he should steady the canoe for the second.

If you are launching the canoe straight out, the bowman boards first at the stern, while the sternman steadies the canoe, and carefully makes his way to the bow, where, with his paddle, he steadies the canoe for the sternman.

Solo boarding from dock or shore is carried out in the same way.

Boarding the canoe is a matter of balance. With experience, balance will become instinctive in the canoeist. He would no sooner step anywhere but in the center of the canoe than he would cross a busy street without looking.

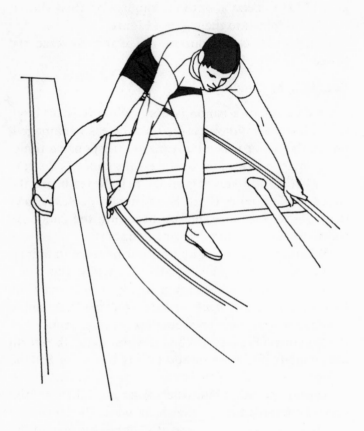

Figure 8
Boarding

Debarking

At a dock, the solo canoeist brings his canoe in parallel to the dock, grasps both gunwales and the painter, and raises himself, resting all his weight on one leg centered over the keel. He then puts his other foot on the dock, transfers all his weight to that leg, and steps up onto the dock, letting go of the gunwales but not the painter.

Tandem paddlers debark the same way. But one canoeist can steady the canoe and hold it against the dock for the other.

When there is no dock, the canoe should be run onto the shore. As it touches the shore, the bowman should step over onto the land, painter in hand. Then, while the bowman holds the canoe, the sternman can also move forward and over the bow onto land.

If there is only one canoeist, he should make his way forward and step onto land, holding the bow painter all the while.

Loading the Canoe

If the canoe is parallel to the shore or dock, the packs can be loaded by both canoeists from the shore, or the bowman can put the packs within reach of the stern-man, who is already in the canoe, so that the latter can stow them amidships.

When the canoe is launched end on, the sternman hands the packs to the bowman, who is already in the canoe. When the packs are properly stowed amidships, the bowman can take his proper place and the stern-man can get into the canoe.

If there are three persons in the party, the center passenger should place the packs fore and aft of him, always maintaining balance.

If there is only one canoeist, his packs should still be placed amidships. Of course, the packs should be loaded before the canoeist gets into the canoe, but it may be necessary for him to rearrange the packs when he gets in.

The pack weight should be distributed evenly, with packs set low and snug and, if there is a prospect of rain, covered with a tarp. The weight in the canoe should always be toward the center and low. If rapids or rough water are the prospect, all packs and gear should be tied to the gunwales or thwarts with rope.

Changing Position

It is inadvisable to change position in a canoe without first landing the canoe on the shore. But sometimes it is necessary. When this movement is unavoidable, it is necessary to move slowly, and only one paddler should be in motion at any one time.

The exchange should be carried out as follows. The bowman lays his paddle in the bilges behind him,

Figure 9
Changing Position

grasps both gunwales, rises, and steps back. He then sits down amidships in the bilges and rests his paddle blade on the water, using the *paddle brace*—the paddler reaches out and rests the blade of his paddle flat on the water to give a third point of contact—and thereby stabilizing the canoe.

The sternman then moves forward, bent over and resting his weight over the keel. He holds onto the gunwales *at all times*. When he has made his way forward, he braces the canoe for the bowman to back to the stern. (Figure 9)

6

Paddling
Techniques

When the Indian paddled, he kneeled and sat on the inner sides of his feet with his weight as low as possible. Today, however, it is more common (and more comfortable) to sit, and paddling from a sitting position will be found to be quite safe in all but the roughest water. For safety, the lower the center of gravity the better, and in rough water the Indian's position is the safest: kneeling low in the canoe amidships. Variations are common: kneeling low in the hull, on one knee, sitting. In calm water it is safe, for the expert, even to paddle standing up.

The little tricks of paddling come with practice. The novice is apt to put all his strength and weight into the stroke and soon tires himself out. The expert takes it easier, keeping a steady pace. He grips the paddle so that his lower arm is almost straight out when beginning the stroke, and he leans forward so that the paddle is nearly vertical, the shaft inclining the least bit in his direction. He allows his whole body to work in the stroke, and he wastes no energy on a stroke once his lower hand reaches his hip; this way he will last longer than the man who is haphazard about his paddling and uses only his arms.

The slow pull with a sweeping recovery is not very efficient. The best stroke, and one not hard to master, is a short stroke with a quick recovery. With this technique the expert is able to make two strokes to the amateur's one. It is not only more speedy and efficient than a long, slow stroke, but it is less tiring as well. The quick recovery almost eliminates loss of momentum, giving the canoe a steady movement ahead and maximum results for the energy expended. Then, too, the quick, short stroke takes advantage of the spring of the blade, which helps shoot the paddle forward, ready for the next stroke. When momentum is at a premium, as, for example, when you are fighting current or strong wind, the quick stroke is especially effective and must be used.

The paddle exerts maximum pressure at the start of the stroke, and the power diminishes rapidly as the paddle approaches the canoeist's side and ends quickly thereafter. A stroke continued behind the paddler serves more to pull down the stern than to add to the forward motion, giving the canoe a bobbing action, since the paddle is then lifting water instead of pulling the canoe *through* the water.

Figure 10
Bow Stroke

Paddling Strokes

There are a number of ways to paddle a canoe, but all methods are variations or modifications of a few basic strokes. Using those that follow, you can handle a canoe with skill and precision. Variations, as well as combinations, of these strokes can be worked out as you become expert.

Bow Stroke. This stroke is the mainstay of the bowman, and it is used to move the canoe forward. (Figure 10)

Grasp the paddle at the grip with one hand and the shaft just above the blade with the other, keeping the upper arm bent and the lower arm straight. Pull your lower arm to the rear and push forward across your body with your upper arm, guiding the paddle aft, parallel with the keel and close to the gunwale, until your lower arm is just slightly back of your hip—*no farther*.

On the recovery relax both arms and bring the blade back to the starting position of the stroke, with the blade feathered so that it is flat and close to the surface.

When the bow stroke is done correctly, both arms do an equal amount of work. A slight rotation of your trunk and shoulders will aid in the smooth delivery.

Backwater Stroke. The backwater stroke is nearly the reverse of the bow stroke and is used by both bowman and sternman simply to stop the forward movement of the canoe or to propel it backward. (Figure 11)

Put the paddle in the water well behind you. Push the lower arm forward and pull the upper arm back, bringing the paddle forward, parallel with the keel and close to the gunwale, until the lower arm is fully extended. On the recovery feather the blade, in the same manner as in the bow stroke.

An alternate way to hold the canoe steady when the forward motion of the canoe is only slight is to thrust the paddle into the water just ahead of your position and hold it vertically, with the paddle's shaft

Figure 11
Backwater Stroke

braced against the gunwale and its blade faced against the direction of movement. In this steady position you can also make repeated short backwater strokes to move the canoe astern.

Draw Stroke. The draw stroke is used by both canoeists to move the canoe sideward, toward the blade. It differs from the bow stroke in that the paddle movement is at right angles to the keel of the canoe instead of parallel to it. (Figure 12)

Starting the stroke a comfortable arm's reach from the canoe, directly to your side, draw the paddle toward you, relaxing your effort when the shaft is about six inches from the gunwale.

Take care that the paddle is not carried under the canoe or jammed into the gunwale. On the recovery bring the blade back to the starting position above the water, or give the blade a half turn and slice it through the water.

Figure 12
Draw Stroke

Both bowman and sternman can use this stroke at the same time to execute a pivot turn, or any part of a turn. The draw stroke can also be modified to give movement in any direction by combining it with the bow stroke. In a stormy wind or current, for example, the tendency to move off course can be eliminated by reaching out at an angle to counteract the force of wind or current and executing a draw-bow stroke.

Pushover Stroke. As the name implies, the pushover stroke moves the canoe away from the side of the paddler and is the direct opposite of the draw stroke. (Figure 13)

Start the stroke with the paddle blade near the canoe and your upper arm extended over the water. Then push the paddle away from the canoe with your lower arm and pull it toward the canoe with your upper arm. For best results hold your lower arm close to your hip, with your wrist and forearm straight.

Figure 13
Pushover Stroke

As in the draw stroke, paddle recovery can be made by feathering the blade above the water or by slicing it through the water at right angles to the paddler.

The pushover stroke can also be accomplished by levering the blade outward, using the gunwale as a fulcrum. Though this *pry stroke* is an easier method, it is possible to damage the gunwale and the shaft if this stroke is made repeatedly. Consequently use it only when extremely rapid action is necessary.

Like the draw stroke, the pushover stroke can be modified to give the desired angle.

The draw and pushover strokes can be used in combination—one by bowman and the other by sternman —to move the canoe bodily sideward, and they are therefore very useful in fast water, where rapid action may be necessary. In fact, the slower steering strokes will probably be inadequate in fast water because the canoe's reaction will not be quick enough.

Figure 14
Sweep and Reverse Sweep Strokes

Sweep and Reverse Sweep Strokes. Another stroke
that is useful in making full or partial turns is the
sweep stroke, as is its opposite, the reverse sweep.
Both of these strokes come in handy when following
the bends of a stream or maneuvering around rocks
and deadheads, as well as when trying to keep a
straight course in strong winds. (Figure 14)

The full sweep is used by the solo paddler and covers a 180-degree arc, starting at a point ahead and going to a point directly behind him. Sitting amidships, put the paddle in the water ahead of you alongside the hull and swing it in a wide sweep away from the canoe and then back to the stern. The movement is the same as that for the bow stroke, except that both hands are low: the upper hand at the waist and the lower out over the water. The stroke recovery on the full sweep is the same as that used for the bow stroke. Remember to feather the paddle. Repeated full sweeps will pivot the canoe completely in a counterclockwise direction, without moving it forward or backward to any extent, but you can use any part of the 180-degree arc at any time.

For tandem work, the sweep is often modified to the half or quarter sweep, the paddle moving through an arc of 90 or 45 degrees. The bowman finds the quarter sweep especially useful in correcting the direction of the canoe when it is swinging toward the side on which he is paddling. The sternman's quarter sweep will, of course, swing the canoe toward the paddling side.

The exact opposite of the full sweep is the reverse sweep. This stroke starts astern of the paddler and ends ahead of him at the bow. It will turn the canoe in the opposite, clockwise, direction. Reverse quarter and half sweeps will also provide the opposite movement to forward quarter and half sweeps.

J Stroke. The J stroke is used in both solo and tandem paddling almost all the time to keep the canoe on a straight course. Since one cannot paddle beneath the keel, even the regular paddling stroke (the bow stroke), which should be made with the paddle parallel to the keel, tends to turn the canoe away from the paddling side. The J stroke is used to offset this tendency, and it is far more efficient than changing paddling sides every few strokes or using the paddle as a rudder. (Figure 15)

Figure 15
J Stroke

The J stroke is the same as the bow stroke, except that at the halfway point the paddle makes a "J" hook in the water. Begin the stroke ahead and a little to one side. The shaft should be vertical. Draw the blade into the side of the canoe and as much under the keel as possible. When the paddle is almost level with the hip, twist the blade by turning your wrists, so that the blade is at an angle of 45 degrees to the hull.

The last part of the stroke will be made easier and less tiring, especially at first, by allowing the paddle to run along the outwale, using it as a fulcrum.

It is quite likely that each canoeist will find a special variation of the J stroke to suit his own needs. One such way is to bend the upper hand at the wrist when the paddle is almost at the hip, thereby forcing the blade out and toward the surface. All that is necessary is that each canoeist learns one form of J stroke to enable him to correct the swing of the canoe.

On the recovery, the blade is kept flat and close to the water, the leading edge slightly elevated, the arms relaxed.

The J stroke is used by the sternman much of the time when paddling in tandem. The main difference between the sternman's J stroke and the solo J stroke is that while the solo paddler begins with a 45-degree draw stroke, the sternman begins with a regular bow stroke until the paddle is halfway to the hip and then describes a "J" in the water. The reason for this execution is that the sternman is behind the pivotal point (center) of the canoe and needs no diagonal turn until he gets past the pivotal point of the stroke.

The amount of twist the sternman gives the J stroke will vary, depending on water conditions and the amount of correction needed. In tandem work it is up to the sternman to direct the course of the canoe in most cases, and this he must do with his paddle technique.

Sculling Stroke. The sculling stroke is used to move the canoe sideward when quicker movement is desired. (Figure 16)

Place the paddle in an almost vertical position a short way from the canoe and move it back and forth parallel to the canoe, in a movement covering 2–3 feet. For the forward stroke, turn the leading edge of the blade away from the canoe at an angle of about 30 degrees; for the backward stroke, reverse the angle. Repeat this back and forth motion, always making sure

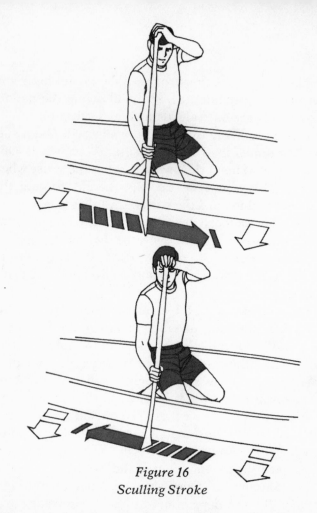

Figure 16
Sculling Stroke

that the forward edge of the blade is at an angle to the canoe. Increase or decrease the angle of the blade depending on the conditions of current, wind, or wave. When solo canoeing, scull toward one end when the other end swings around.

The sculling stroke is very effective for slowing down the canoe in rapids.

Bow Rudder, Stern Rudder, and Cross-Bow Rudder Strokes. Rudder strokes will not work *first* unless the canoe is underway and traveling faster than the current, and *second* when the current is very fast, especially in rapids. (Figure 17) At such times, the draw, pushover and pry, sculling, and sweep strokes are the only effective means of altering course.

Figure 17
Rudder Strokes

The bow rudder moves the bow of the canoe at a sharp angle *toward* the bowman's paddling side. Place the paddle blade in the water at a sharp angle to the bow and hold it there. The canoe will move sharply toward the paddle. To give the stroke more effect, the bowman can brace his lower arm or the heel of his hand against the gunwale, grasping the paddle shaft firmly.

In tandem paddling, if the sternman matches the bowman's bow rudder with a reverse quarter sweep and *stern rudder* (holding the paddle firm in the position gained at the end of the reverse sweep stroke) on the opposite side, there will be even more movement.

To move the bow of the canoe sharply *away* from the bowman's normal paddling side, the *cross-bow rudder* stroke—the opposite of the bow rudder—is used. In this stroke the bowman moves the paddle to the side opposite to the one on which he was paddling and holds it there. As in the bow rudder, the lower forearm or the heel of the hand can be held against the gunwale for more effect. In this stroke, however, the upper hand is held low, braced against the hip, giving more support than when the upper arm is high and forward.

Other paddling strokes suggest themselves to the canoeist as he becomes more expert, but the foregoing are basic and can be used under most conditions.

7

Swift-Water Canoeing

If you travel a river far enough, chances are that sooner or later you will run into rapids. They may first show up as shallower water or be heralded by the appearance of an occasional rock or boulder in midstream, the water coursing past it. It won't be long before you feel the current quicken and detect eddies, rips, swirls, and the presence of dangerous obstructions. You feel the pull or push on the canoe and hear the roar of the rapids as you round a sudden bend. Surging, white, black, there they are as far as you can see.

Can you run them?

Rapids

If this is unfamiliar water, you don't know until you have beached the canoe and gone *on foot* to see. This is the first and most vital rule in white-water canoeing. If you don't know, go and see. The second rule also concerns safety: never run rapids alone. If your canoe is smashed, you must have other canoes handy to take you on. Probably the minimum number of canoes for running rapids is three. Third, always wear a life preserver when you are in white water (see Chapter 9 for details).

A portage or another means of navigation may be necessary for any or all of the paddlers. A smashed canoe, along with the loss of grub and equipment, is a serious matter and must be avoided. If there is the slightest doubt, *portage*. If there is a good chance that you can run the rapids, unload the canoes and carry all the gear through, then make the attempt.

In working through the rapids, keep to the deepest part of the stream; stick to the channel as much as possible. The channel customarily runs from one outside of a bend to another. On straight stretches of river, it is usually in the middle. If one bank is undercut and higher than the other, the water will probably be deeper nearer that shore. If one side is very low, watch out for shallows on that side.

Watch out for muddy water. The obstructions in muddy water will reveal themselves only when they are very pronounced. In clear-water rivers most underwater obstructions will reveal themselves by the lighter color of the water. Where there are rocky places or gravel bars just under the surface, for instance, the water will be yellow and light, while the water around a rock that rises above the surface will show definitely white. If the rapids are strong in these places, the rock will split the current into a distinct "V," with the point of the "V" upstream. The rounded boulder that causes the water to rise over it can be quite as dangerous as the sharp rock that splits the water in a white boil, since it can cause an upset just as easily.

Turbulence, change in water color, change in water speed—these are the danger signals. Avoid all projections. Turn the canoe into the free and deeper part of the channel and pick out what looks like a safe course. Try to avoid waves that are white and foamy; they will be full of air and will not support your canoe as will regular river water. Always watch for rocks, and remember that missing one, even by only a foot or so, will be enough to pass it safely.

Time was when the canoeist paddled his canoe faster than the run of the current to keep control of his craft, steering with the paddle and using the quarter-sweep stroke where needed. This method still has its advocates, but there is no question that by increasing the speed of the canoe you are increasing the hazards, because you will have less control over your movements and less time to make them. It is, therefore, safer to keep the canoe going no faster than the current, in fact, even to slow it up as much as possible. This is where the sculling draw is effective. It allows both directional and lateral control of the canoe. Using the sculling draw, the paddlers can move either the bow, the stern, or the entire canoe from one side to the other.

The ability to move the canoe rapidly and accurately is essential in running rapids. However, when you need to slip the canoe from side to side to take advantage of current and openings, even the sculling draw may prove inadequate. At such times, you should resort to the backwater stroke to slow the canoe and the draw and pushover and pry strokes to give you direction.

With the keel in line with the current, it is quite possible to move the canoe bodily over with the draw and pushover strokes, thereby aligning the canoe to slip through a new opening. An even more valuable trick, however, is the *sideslip*. (Figure 18) Given a strong current, angling the bow of the canoe against the current will result in the canoe's being swept in the opposite direction. Of course, there is a danger in so doing that the canoe will be forced broadside on to the current, and in any sideslipping movement the sternman should be alert to swing the stern to one side to ensure that the canoe keel remains in line with the current.

When navigating heavy rapids, the canoeists should place themselves near the center of the canoe so that the ends of the canoe will rise and fall with the waves. Good balance depends on a low center of gravity, so the paddlers must be low and well braced. They should assume a kneeling position while paddling,

Figure 18
Sideslipping

with toes inward and knees spread out into the bilges. This squat position gives leverage, and the low center of gravity of the paddler in this position makes him almost a part of the canoe.

In the kneeling position, the paddler may rest his rear on his heels or against a thwart, but he should not touch the canoe with any other part of the body. The trunk, shoulders, arms, and paddle must be free to provide balance at all times in fast water.

Added stability can be gained by using a *paddle brace*. When the canoe strikes a heavy wave, the canoeist should place his paddle blade on the surface of the water out and away from the side of the canoe. This "outrigger" effect gives the canoe an additional point of contact with the water and extra stability at a crucial moment.

In all rapids' navigation the bowman has the key role as observer, watching for obstructions and signaling the best course. He should watch for "boils," the patch of swirling water directly below a rock caused by the flow of smooth water over the rock, and "haystacks," the waves caused by fast-moving water's having its momentum checked suddenly when it comes upon deeper, calmer water. It is here the bowman must really keep alert, calling the moves and avoiding the rocks and obstructions. Meanwhile, the sternman must control the canoe and steady it. Neither paddler's skills are easily acquired, and continual practice is necessary before any "real" rapids are run.

The Run

As the canoeists slip into the current, "slow" is the watchword. They scull the canoe and work into the free channel with as much control as possible. With a course in mind, the canoeists feel the surge of the current and then plunge forward. Once committed, they grip their paddles hard and keep their eyes open. Down they go, faster and faster. The bowman has his job cut out for him. He sees two rocks with just enough leeway between them for the canoe to pass. The bowman makes a strong "in-draw," swinging the canoe to the left to miss the danger spot, and the sternman follows with a strong "out-draw" to bring his end of the canoe into line. The canoe swings into the current, straightens out between the two huge boulders, passes them, and then is caught in a surge of raging water that veers to the right. Both paddlers have already taken this into consideration, and, with the sternman sculling strongly, the canoe sweeps away from the rock and into deep, boiling water.

So far so good. But just ahead several other rocks loom up suddenly. The bowman angles and cuts into the current, the sternman follows his lead with a draw stroke, and they are again racing through the boulder-strewn river, barely missing the rocks.

Suddenly they leave the white water behind and swing with the steep gradient into a wide bend where the water swirls along a rock wall and then into deeper, calmer water. They have swept safely through a half mile of boiling water. The worst is over. They've covered the half mile of river in minutes. It's hard to believe, so, shipping paddles for a moment, the two tired but exuberant men reach out and shake hands.

Upstream Paddling

Upstream paddling is more difficult and certainly not as popular as downstream canoeing, but some-times the canoeists have no choice but to travel up-stream. To make best upstream progress, pick a course through water that offers the least resistance; that is, water that is not too shallow. Keep near shore, if pos-sible, for there the current is usually more moderate, and often the water is deeper than it is in midstream. The exception to the rule is the outside of a bend. There the water is deeper, but also the current is faster, and you should keep to slower water. Look for eddies; they will allow you to rest a little, and you can get out of them fast and pick up speed. In fact, many back eddies flow upstream. These should be utilized in all upstream paddling. (See also the next chapter, on poling and tracking.)

8

Poling, Tracking, and Wading

The canoeist can still use his canoe even when the water is running too fast or too dangerously for him to paddle it. On such occasions, it is often possible to avoid the portage by poling, tracking, or wading.

Poling

Poling is a technique that is useful for going upstream, especially in rapids or fast water. Indeed, the experienced poler will be able to propel his canoe upstream in conditions that make paddling impossible. Basically, the technique involves the canoeist's applying force to a pole to move the canoe in the direction desired. (Figure 19)

The pole itself should be tapered, 10–12 feet long (though some like longer poles), have a diameter of about 1½ inches at the tip, and be smoothed of all stubs. I have found that a slender spruce or maple sapling, one that is fairly straight and evenly tapered, makes a good canoe pole. Never use the paddle for poling except in an emergency.

The pole can be fitted with a pointed iron socket, or shoe, at the heavy end. But most poling can be done with the staff just as it comes from the woods, although the brooming may have to be trimmed off the tip from time to time when you're doing a lot of poling.

Since it is necessary to rest the pole on the bottom of the river, it will be found that it is difficult to pole

Figure 19
Poling

in water more than 3½ feet deep. However, it is usually possible to find a channel that is not too deep, especially since fast water is often shallow, especially near the shore.

One of the great advantages of poling is the fact that it allows the poler to snub, or stop, the canoe at any time. All he does is angle the pole in against the bottom of the river and against the current and, with legs braced, hold the canoe in position. This technique is very valuable in downstream canoeing, for it enables the paddler to inspect the next stretch of water, rest, or prepare to move the canoe in some particular direction.

Successful poling depends a great deal on balance. The canoe, being light, moves over the water in response to the canoeist's "climbing" his pole. Consequently, when the poler stands, as is usually the case, and once the initial direction has been chosen by the poler's snubbing his pole (at some distance to the side, ahead, astern) and beginning to draw his canoe over to where the point is, the feet are used to steer the canoe, since they, along with one leg if it is braced against a thwart, are the only parts of the body in contact with the canoe. Thus the poler must learn to adjust his weight and foot position to align the canoe properly as he draws it over to where he snubbed his pole.

To pole you can either stand or kneel in the canoe. (You can get more power by standing.) Hold the pole firmly. Going upstream, drop the pole down beside you, align the canoe with your feet, and thrust backward with the pole, climbing it hand over hand. Repeat the movement.

In downstream poling and where the current is not too strong, drag the pole, pressed firmly into the river bottom at an angle, behind you for the desired effect.

Poling calls for balance, quick reflexes, and, in the two-man poling procedures, close teamwork. For two-man poling upstream, it's usually best to work the poles on opposite sides of the canoe. But each situation demands trial and error. There is no one rule. I recommend that the canoeists also try poling on the same side on the first stretch of rough water.

Poling is the answer when paddling is out of the question. But it will be found that the most successful progress is made, in tandem canoeing, when one man (the sternman usually) poles and the other paddles.

The combination of pole and paddle usually ensures continuous forward momentum and considerable maneuverability.

Tracking

You may encounter stretches of water where the pitch of the rapids is so severe that the canoe is best handled by ropes from shore, a method called tracking. (Figure 20) To track, the canoeists go ashore at the head

Figure 20
Tracking

or the foot of swift rapids and "line" the canoe through the water with ropes attached to its bow and stern. One man can track the canoe, but two will handle it more successfully, especially if the water is rough and the current fast.

For most streams, each tracking line need be no more than 50 feet long. Better for the larger streams, however, are lines 100 feet long, pliable and well treated with beeswax and turpentine for easy handling. The stern line is tied to the stern seat or thwart, and the bow line to the front seat or thwart, with a bowline knot.

When the lines are attached to the bow and stern thwarts or seats, however, there is a danger, especially in rivers with diverse currents, that the canoe will suddenly be swept across the current. At that time, because the lines are exerting pressure on the upper parts of the canoe, there is a danger that the canoe will be overturned.

You can protect yourself against this possibility by using a *towing bridle*. (Figure 21) Make a large loop in the end of the towing line (use a running bowline knot) and slip it over the stern of the canoe. Set the loop so that its middle is behind the stern thwart, and then lock it there by slipping the paddle blade between the line and the thwart. The line will now exert pressure at the keel line, and there will be little danger of the canoe's being upset by the cross-pull of a line attached to the upperworks. Whether tracking upstream or downstream, head the stern into the current.

Before beginning to track, make sure the canoe is loaded properly, with packs well balanced, tied down, and placed amidships and low to keep the canoe from bucking in a strong current and shipping water.

When tracking upstream and where the river is comparatively free of obstructions, both canoeists can walk along the shore and handle the ropes. But where there is danger of the canoe's foundering, one man

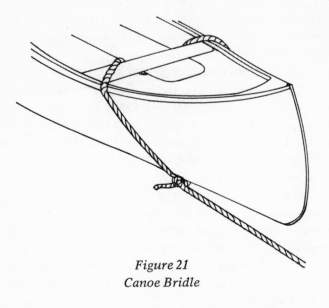

Figure 21
Canoe Bridle

should remain in the canoe to paddle and guide while the other does the tracking from the shore, handling both lines. To track upstream, push the canoe out into the current until there is a strong pull on the stern line. As the stern line tightens, bring the bow line into play to keep the canoe in line with the current, and then proceed to track the canoe upstream. It is especially easy, when tracking upstream, to let the stern swing broadside on to the current, and this should be guarded against; likewise, going downstream. If the canoe does get caught and ships water, bring it to shore, drain it, and put it out again.

Wading

The canoe can also be pushed or pulled where the going is rough and the water not too deep if the canoeists leave the canoe and wade through the water, guiding their craft. In narrow streams and where there are not only rocks and logs but fallen trees obstructing the stream, this is about the only way to move the canoe, other than by portaging. Most canoeists avoid such waters, but if they should be met, they must be covered somehow.

Conclusion

Ingenuity and trial and error really count when navigating rapids and troublesome water. The more practice you have before meeting these situations, the better you will cope with them. There is always a way, and the easiest procedure is usually the best one. Paddle, portage, pole, track, push, pull, and the rapids can be covered. A little reconnoitering beforehand will usually indicate the way, especially if you remember the most important rule: when in doubt—*portage.*

9

Portaging
and Backpacking

As a canoe camper you will have to do some portaging and backpacking at some time or another. It can be fun or work, depending on how you go about it. To make sure it is the former, carry the right sort of pack and learn the little intricacies of handling a canoe on dry land.

Portaging

If you possess a *portage yoke,* a piece of wood shaped to fit your head and shoulders and easily fixed to the gunwales, put it in place; otherwise, lash the two paddles across the thwarts so that the blades will lie across your shoulders when the canoe is hoisted over-

Figure 22
Yoke and Tumpline

head. When yoke or paddles are in place, turn the canoe over. Take hold of both gunwales near one end and lift the end of the canoe until you can walk under it. Move backward until you can lower the yoke onto your shoulders, at which time the canoe should be in balance, on your shoulders and off the ground. (Figure 22)

Alternately, one man can set the canoe on his shoulders by lifting it onto one shoulder—in the way described for the short carry—and letting it flop over onto both shoulders. (Figure 23)

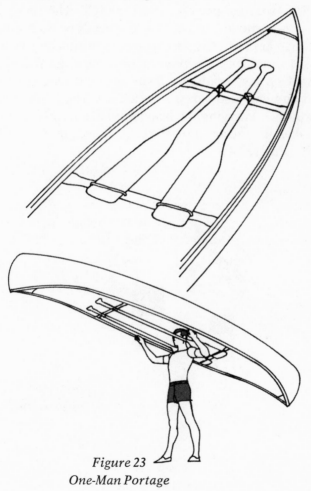

Figure 23
One-Man Portage

The point of balance is just in front of the canoe center so that the canoe will tilt back and down. It is easier to pull down the front of the canoe than push it up, and you will be able to see where you are going. That way, too, you can fit a *tumpline,* a leather head strap attached to the yoke, to enable your head and neck to assist in the carry. Properly in balance, the canoe can be held in place with one hand.

Pads, often made of rolled up sweaters or other clothing, set in place under the paddles will eliminate most of the discomfort encountered on a long portage.

The two-man portage also is simple. The canoe is lifted, one end at a time, over the heads of both men. The man at the stern rests the stern deck and gunwales on his shoulders; the man at the bow rests the bow thwart on his shoulders. Both men can now see the trail and can also carry a pack each. The front man, however, is carrying the heavier load, and this should be taken into account when the pack weight is distributed. (Figure 24)

Figure 24
Two-Man Portage

Backpacking

The first rule on a canoe trip is the fewer the packs, the better, although there is no point in trying to overload the packs just to keep their number down. One large pack per man is usually sufficient, but if it is not, use two.

Packs should be as few as possible and well packed to simplify portaging and to save time in collecting equipment at each portage. Packsacks make the job easier; at the portage the canoeist merely lifts the pack from the canoe, transfers it to his back, and is on his way.

All packs are fitted with shoulder straps of some kind, but in addition the canoe camper may want to make use of a tumpline, excellent for handling heavy and bulky gear. In the days of the fur brigade, the tumpline was classed as a necessity. The *voyageur* was pretty much in the backpacking business and wanted to make his trips count, no matter what the load. Today, however, with lighter packs and shorter trips, a tumpline is not a necessity, but for many it remains an asset.

The backpack tumpline consists of two soft leather straps, each about 8 feet long, and a leather head strap 1–2 inches wide. The equipment is placed in packs or wrapped in a tarpaulin—the heavier pieces below and the lighter above—and bound together by the straps. The load is then held together at the top by, and attached to, the head strap.

The broad head strap is placed against the forehead, *above* rather than *on* it, and the body is bent forward to assume a comfortable position that both balances and distributes the weight of the pack. Loads up to 300 pounds and more can be transported this way, mostly over short distances, and the tumpline is therefore handy for the hardened outdoorsman. But until the very strong neck muscles get used to the weight on the head, the occasional cruiser will find the tumpline-carry method very strenuous and should probably stick to a 90-pound load. Even for the occasional canoe camper, however, some head-strap arrangement is advised for a long cruise with considerable equipment.

If the portage is apt to be long, the canoe and gear should be moved in relays, taking part of the load part way, then returning for the remainder. Moving the equipment part way and in small amounts will prove less taxing than carrying the entire load all at once and all the way. It also renders the equipment safer from foraging animals.

Take only as much as you can conveniently carry. Stop to rest before getting overtired. Pick your path carefully, looking ahead as you hike along. Avoid brush. In most canoe country there are trails of a sort. Do your best to find the portage: a path well used by others before you. When in doubt, look for notches in the brush and trees, search for blazes and the telltale paint marks made by previous canoes. It is poor economy to push blindly through the brush when there is an easier trail to follow.

Where brush and trees are bothersome, clear the trail for both yourself and the next party. On overgrown paths the packer can often tell by the "feel" of the trail whether he is on it or not. Keeping to the trail will save you considerable time. Always consult your compass and maps to be certain of your direction.

When you feel yourself stumbling and trying to increase your speed, you are going too fast. Keep a relaxed but consistent pace. If you're on a long trip that involves many portages, be ready for exertion. Develop wind and limb by doing as much walking as possible before the trip. The city, as well as the country, offers unlimited opportunities for building up muscle and wind by taking long jaunts. Hike a little every day for some time before a big outing, gradually extending your walks so that you can stay on your feet for two or three hours at a time, keeping up a steady pace. Easy walking and hiking can be fun in themselves for a family or for a lone hiker.

Types of Packs

Many packs are produced for the average camper. (Figure 25) One of the best—favored, after much experimentation, by lumberjacks and woodsmen—is the *Duluth,* or Northwestern, type of pack, several variations of which are available. One popular variety is made of heavy duck, and it offers a roomy pack with one or two outside bellows pockets for smaller articles. Drawstrings are fitted to the top of the pack to keep it closed tightly, and three straps on the outside are used to close the pack cover. Two wide web or leather straps are used for shoulder carrying, and a web tumpline can be fitted to the packsack for head carrying if desired. With both shoulder straps and a head strap, the camper is able to carry a really large load. Sizes vary in this bag, but I have found that the No. 3 is a good choice for most canoe trips.

The *pack cloth* is also a handy carrier on the canoe cruise. It is a fair-sized piece of tarp into which the

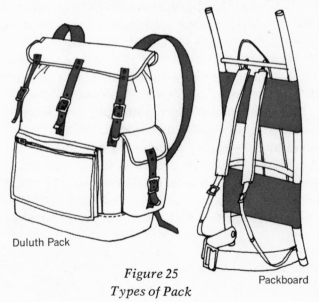

Duluth Pack

Figure 25
Types of Pack

Packboard

duffel is dumped. The ends are pulled together and attached to the tumpline with rope or straps. This pack is very practical. When opened at camp, everything is in plain sight; it is quickly packed and tied again when camp is broken. Personal items can be stowed in a small rucksack, either carried separately or wrapped up with the other equipment in the pack cloth.

The pack cloth can be supplemented by the waterproof groundsheet from your tent, if the sheet is not sewed into the tent. The sheet can be used to carry such items as your air mattress, the tent itself, and your sleeping bag. Roll up the contents into a tight pack, starting with one corner of the cloth and wrapping with the idea of keeping the contents waterproof and packed so that they will not move at all. Then bind the sheet with a strap or rope and carry the roll over your shoulder.

The trapper-type woven *pack basket* can also be used, but it is not waterproof unless covered with a tarp or placed in a packsack. Used as a liner for the Duluth packsack, the pack basket is excellent, especially when carrying canned foods and the like: the liner prevents the sharper articles from gouging your back. The basket is not a necessity, however, and can be eliminated where weight is a problem.

Another favored pack is the *packboard* or pack frame, which is a frame onto which you can tie your sack. The frame is made either of wood slats or of a light metal such as aluminum, and it is fitted with shoulder straps. The pack frame is much favored by mountaineers and is undergoing continual improvement. It is, however, first and foremost a walker's sack, and while it can be used on a canoe cruise, with such regular packsacks as the Duluth available, I would pick the latter for its all-around convenience.

10

Canoe and Paddle Repair and Care

When you go canoeing, especially in the wilderness, there is always the chance of the canoe's being damaged. Be prepared for this contingency: carry a repair kit.

Secure a complete kit for emergency repairs in a waterproof bag beneath a deck. A simple kit usually is inexpensive and contains all the materials necessary to do a satisfactory job on the canoe, along with instructions for using it. You can obtain one from a canoe manufacturer, canoe outfitter, or canoe shop, and it should always be part and parcel of the canoeist's equipment.

Canoe Repair

Your repair kit should always contain nitrate dope or fingernail polish and adhesive tape. With tape and dope you can repair almost any canoe. For example, say you must repair a rent in a wood-and-canvas canoe. Make sure the hull is dry. Cut off two generous pieces of the tape and place them tightly over both sides of the damaged section—inside the canoe and out. For an even tighter seal, apply more tape over the same spot. Dip your finger in the dope and smear it on the new patch and over the edges of the damaged area. The dope will dry immediately, and such a repair, if the puncture is not too severe, will render the canoe waterproof again and hold for some time.

Emergency repairs to canvas canoes can also be made with a good grade marine glue and the small pieces of canvas that come with the repair kit for this type of canoe. Square off the canvas rip. Cut two patches of cloth an inch larger than the hole to be covered. Fray the edges of the patches for better adhesion and appearance. Work one patch and some waterproof glue in underneath the canvas. Allow to set. Glue the outside patch to the canoe. Allow to set. Fill in the edges of the rent with canvas filler. Allow to set. Apply varnish or dope. If it is impossible to work a patch in under the canvas, put one on top only. Filler takes a long time to set and should not be used on the trail. In all cases on a trip, use layers of tape and dope.

Small tears in a wood-and-canvas canoe can also be repaired with *waterproof liquid cement*, another handy item for the repair kit. Dry the damaged spot well, fill the tear with liquid cement, allow it to dry, and then apply a second coat.

Lacking the manufactured adhesive, you can substitute *pitch* or *resin* from evergreen trees such as spruce or pine, and with it do a very satisfactory job. Pure resin, however, is quite sticky. It will do in a pinch, but it is rather messy to apply and does have a tendency to harden and crack when exposed to cold water. It is much better mixed with a little cooking fat and applied hot. Therefore, to lend the pitch the right consistency, mix it in the proportion of six parts resin to one part cooking fat. Heat. While still warm, apply the mixture to the damaged spot and allow it to harden.

Chewing gum makes a good sealer for minor repairs on any type of canoe. It should be applied when soft and allowed to harden. Daubed on both sides of a rent, chewing gum will often make a strong and lasting emergency repair.

Small rents or leaks in an aluminum canoe can be sealed with the *liquid aluminum compound* that comes in tubes and is available in most hardware stores. The surface of the metal canoe around the leak should be flattened out by holding a block of wood against the dented side and carefully pounding on the bulged side with the padded butt end of your hatchet. Smooth the surface over as well as possible and then apply the liquid to the leak. If one coat seems insufficient, allow it to set and then add another.

A good aluminum-canoe repair job also can be made while on the cruise by using *aluminum plastic-wood paste,* available from canoe manufacturers and canoe shops. This plastic-wood paste is applied directly to cracks and small holes or, in the case of larger holes, daubed over a fiber patch. It is best applied in thin layers. Allow time for each layer to set before adding another. The spot to be covered should be sanded between each application of the paste, and the finished patch should also be sanded to a smooth finish.

Contrary to general opinion, *welding is not advisable* in repairing aluminum canoes; the heat will render the damaged spot brittle and leave a soft area of aluminum around it.

Riveting an aluminum patch makes a lasting repair, if the patch overlaps the crack or hole by an inch or more, but this repair is best made in a permanent camp. A loose rivet in an aluminum canoe can be tightened by holding a stone against the outside head and striking against the inside with the butt end of the hatchet. If a rivet is pulling out, it can be replaced with one a little larger: chisel off the rivet's outer head, punch it out, and replace it with one of heavier gauge.

Dents can be smoothed out by holding a block of wood against the dented side and pounding out the bulged side with the butt end of the hatchet. Wood-and-canvas, aluminum, and fiber-glass canoes can be repaired with a *fiber-glass repair kit,* which is very inexpensive, contains complete directions and materials, and requires no special tools. The epoxy resin and hardener used for fiber-glass repairs may need to be heated; for it seldom sets below 60 degrees. When not used with the fiber-glass cloth and mat, the resin will serve as regular glue.

Permanent repairs on any canoe can be made when the cruise is over, or when there is a canoe rental shop in the vicinity.

Canoe Care

Canoes spend less time in the water than out of it, and therefore special care of them is necessary at all times.

Canoe racks, a half-canoe length apart, are necessary to keep the canoe off the ground, and the rack should be sheltered from wind, sun, and rain while still allowing ventilation. (Figure 26) In winter the canoe should be stored inside, but by then it must be completely dry.

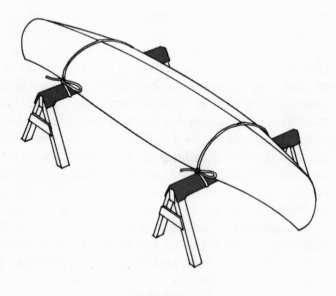

Figure 26
Canoe Storage

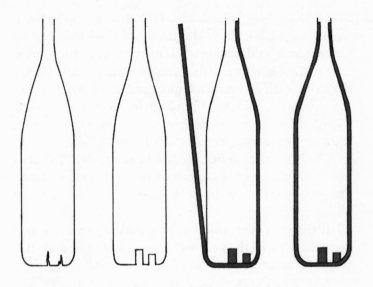

Figure 27
Paddle Repairs

The canoe should be stored bottom up, and after each trip it should be repaired, ready for the next cruise.

Varnish and paint should be applied as necessary —for all bare spots permit moisture absorption—but only after the places needing a coat have been sanded. "Only put on as much as you take off" is a good rule.

All makeshift repairs made en route should be checked and more lasting repairs undertaken if the temporary repairs are not holding up.

Paddle Repair

If it is felt that the damage to the paddle is insufficient to justify throwing it away, repairs can be carried out. (Figure 27)

Split blades can be repaired quite easily. Trim off any superfluous splinters and, using waterproof glue, glue the fractured pieces together. Bind up the paddle until the glue dries, and protect the split edge with wood strips, applied singly. (Be sure to extend the strips 1–2 inches above the throat of the blade and to plane, sand, and varnish this new "lamination" to a smooth finish.) Alternately, a split paddle blade can be repaired with waterproof glue and tape. First apply the glue at the split, then bind the blade with cord until the glue has dried, and then apply the tape tightly, touching the end of the tape with a dab of glue.

The broomed paddle blade can be repaired by tacking on a thin strip of copper or tin, if available, along the broomed tip, or the brooming can be trimmed off with a knife.

If the split is too wide to be glued together, cut out the split and fill the hole with a wood plug and plastic wood. Sand and varnish to ensure a good finish.

Snapped shafts also can be repaired. If the break is reasonably "clean," joint the two pieces with a lap joint. Cut and glue the joint. Bind it until it is dry, and then, if it will not interfere with paddling, apply a leather collar to the shaft to strengthen the joint. The lap joint must be clean, so it may be necessary to shorten the paddle to make the joint.

If the break is frayed, trim to fit and glue as above.

Paddle Care

To add to the paddle's life and to prevent damage to it and the outwale when the two come in contact, the shaft, for 8–12 inches above the throat of the blade, can be fitted with a leather collar or reinforced with a layer or two of machinists' tape. Likewise, a copper tip can be fitted to the blade to prevent splitting and brooming, but most canoeists dislike metal tips since they catch and hold dirt and moisture, are rather unsightly, and are noisy in use.

A high-quality, well-made paddle will last for years with reasonable care. But always use the paddle as a paddle, never as a pry. Paddles should be kept well varnished. Marine spar varnish should be applied in several *thin* coats from time to time. Sand the surface well with fine-grade sandpaper before each coat. Applied to the blade, especially, varnish will keep moisture absorption to a minimum as well as keep the tip from brooming. When your paddle becomes worn in places, be sure to cover these spots with varnish (after first sanding them), because unprotected wood will deteriorate.

Note, however, that many experienced canoeists prefer an unvarnished shaft, and some of the best paddles come this way. On a canoe trip of any duration, using a paddle with a varnished shaft may well cause blisters. An unvarnished but smooth shaft will keep blisters to a minimum. If you buy a paddle with a varnished shaft, apply varnish remover and then sand and polish it.

Keep wet paddles out of the hot sun, and when you're not using them, store them hanging up rather than lying flat. If paddles are left lying on the ground, only one side will dry and there will be shrinkage and consequent warping on that side; people may well step on them; and, last but not least, in the northern states and Canada porcupines will be tempted to chew the salty shafts.

11

Canoe Safety

The canoe is a safe craft. This may come as a surprise to many, but it is true nevertheless. Balance is the primary concern. With proper balance, the occupants of the canoe will have little trouble riding out most wind, wave, and water conditions. The key to safety is the *side-weight distribution:* keep weight distributed equally and as low as possible so that the canoe rides on an even keel, level and trim in the water.

The second factor in canoe safety is the canoe itself. You should always seek expert advice in choosing the size and type of canoe to fit your needs, but as a basic rule we can say that you should choose the largest canoe that fits your requirements: the larger the canoe, the greater the capacity, the faster the speed, the shallower the water you can float in, and the *greater the stability.*

The canoeist should dress lightly, especially about the feet, so that he can take care of himself if the canoe overturns or he falls overboard. But the seasoned canoeist rarely upsets. He gets to know how to handle his craft under all circumstances. He feels instinctively how the canoe is acting and counters with his know-how to keep it safe and afloat.

The safety of your food and equipment, even of your own life, depends on how the canoe is loaded and handled and on how the bowman and sternman cooperate. The canoeists must work together or trouble will surely develop. If one of the canoeists is a novice, it is a good idea to have the experienced man at the stern and the less skilled man in the bow, because the sternman acts as the "captain" of the canoe. He steers the canoe, directs the side on which to paddle, and supervises loading, unloading, pushing off from shore, and landing.

Canoe handling is easy to learn. The novice should first watch his instructor, then ask questions, and finally practice as much as he can. His first ventures in a canoe should be made on a sheltered body of water, when the water is fairly calm. Then, when he has built up his confidence, he can launch out into more ambitious undertakings, perhaps practicing in moving water to learn how to cope with currents. Finally, before any canoeist embarks on a long or demanding canoe trip, he should work out with his canoe on some nearby river or lake to get the feel of his craft again and to harden up his muscles, and he should also take it easy on the first few days of the long trip. Sore muscles make canoeing most unpleasant.

Weight Distribution

Pack and human weight should be distributed so that the canoe rides on an even keel, and the weight will therefore be distributed according to the number of canoeists and wind and water conditions.

The general rule is that during rough weather, the weight should be in the center so that the canoe ends are free to ride over the waves while the center remains stable with a low center of gravity.

One-Man Canoeing. In calm water, the solo canoeist will sit on the stern seat. His gear will be stored amidships. In rough water, he will sit or kneel amidships. If there is a head wind, he will sit just forward of amidships, to keep his bow down and stern high; if there is a following wind, he will sit just astern of amidships, to keep his stern down and bow high.

Two-Man Canoeing. In calm water, the gear will be

stowed amidships, the paddlers at either end. In rough water, the paddlers will sit close together amidships. (Figure 28)

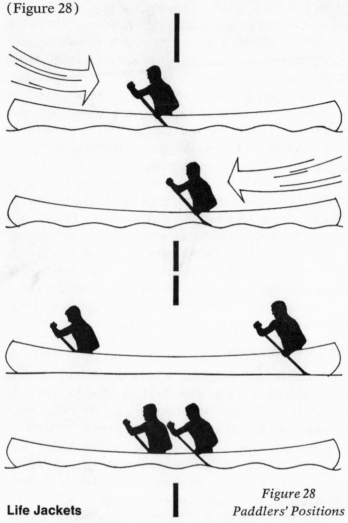

Life Jackets

Figure 28
Paddlers' Positions

In canoeing, as in any water sport, it is a minimum requirement that all participants be able to swim. Even though the canoe is a very safe craft, you cannot know when or under what circumstances you may have to swim—and swim for your life. So as added safeguards wear lightweight shoes or boots that will not pull you down, and carry life jackets.

In fact, the carrying of a life jacket in the canoe for each passenger is imperative. The cushion-type preserver is *not* effective. It is easily punctured and will often float out of reach. One good preserver is the Coast Guard-approved (it will say so on the package) type of life jacket that supports the neck, but it is not entirely comfortable. Whether the experienced canoeist should wear a life jacket in the canoe is up to him, but children or beginning canoeists should wear preservers at all times. In rough water, especially in rapids, all canoeists should have life jackets on.

Self-Rescue

With an Upright Canoe. As a canoeist, and especially as a beginner, you may fall overboard without capsizing your canoe. If you do, make a grab for the gunwale, thwart, seat, or whatever point of the canoe is near you as you go over or as you surface. The canoe is your life preserver: stay with it, hold onto it, but be careful not to capsize it. *Do not try to scramble into the canoe.* You will only capsize it. Make sure of your grip on the canoe—wind, rapids, or the current can easily take it out of your reach—and swim with it, pushing it toward the nearer shore. If the canoe does elude you, swim slowly to shore and recover the canoe later; it will beach itself farther down the river or lake.

A safety precaution to take in case of an upset in rapids, when you still have a grip on the canoe, is to move to the upstream end of the canoe so you will not get caught between the canoe and the rocks. Then hold onto one side of the end so that, if the canoe rams a rock, you will not be thrown against the end. (Figure 29) This maneuver also applies to an upset along a rocky shore on a windy lake. The canoe will hold you up, and you can guide it more easily to a safe landing spot when riding at the stern and protect yourself as well.

The best place to board is toward the center. Pull the canoe close and tip the near side down toward

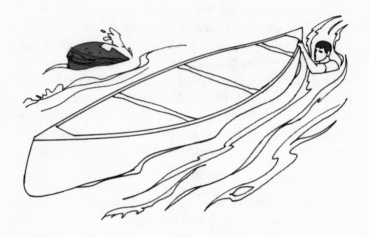

Figure 29
Using the Canoe as a Liferaft

you. Then reach across it, grasp the far gunwale with one hand and the near gunwale with the other, get up near the surface by kicking your legs vigorously, and pull yourself up and over, kicking hard to help force yourself up. Continue to press hard on the far gunwale to prevent the canoe's capsizing and drag yourself over the canoe until you are in a position of balance and can roll over on your back and assume a sitting position. (Figure 30)

If the canoe is too wide to grasp the far gunwale, grip one of the thwarts as far back as possible. With a strong up and down kick, pull yourself up and over, do a quarter turn, and sit down in the canoe. Be sure to pull yourself up far enough to feel that most of your weight is on the thwart, so that the canoe will not overturn while you are boarding it.

If neither of these methods is possible, you can maneuver aboard, using the bilge of the canoe. Bring the canoe to you, place both hands in the near bilge,

Figure 30
Self-Boarding (I)

press down hard, and kick yourself up over the canoe. Keep your head low when boarding, and when the canoe is far enough under you, roll over and pull yourself to a sitting position. (Figure 31) If the packs are

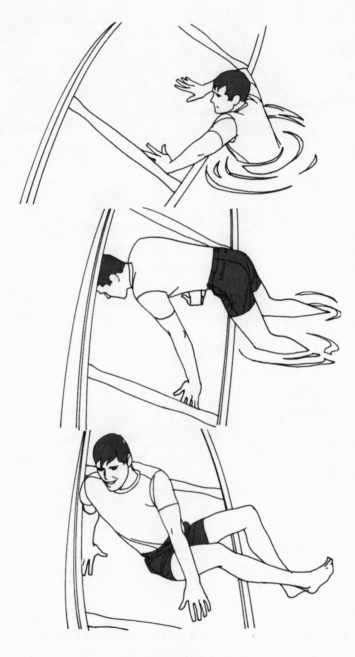

Figure 31
Self-Boarding (II)

amidships, you will have to move closer to the stern or bow.

When one man is in the canoe already, he should sit in the bilge amidships on the side away from the man in the water, thereby steadying the canoe while the swimmer climbs aboard. If both paddlers are in the water, the second one to board should hold onto the gunwale amidships on the opposite side to the one boarding, in order to steady the canoe.

With a Capsized Canoe. If the canoe capsizes, the same basic rule obtains: stay with the craft if at all possible. All wood-and-canvas and most metal and fiber-glass canoes will support you and will not sink. Do not swim away from the canoe. You will be much safer and also be able to recover the canoe if you stay with it.

Should the paddles be lost in an upset on open water, the canoe can be hand-paddled to shore or to shallow water by grasping the gunwale with one hand and paddling with the other. Use both hand and fore-arm when paddling this way.

If your canoe is overturned, swimming with it is usually an easy way to reach shore. Hold onto the bottom with one hand and swim with the other, kicking your legs and paddling with your free hand. Employing the canoe's natural buoyancy—using the canoe as a life preserver—you can rest as often as necessary and rescue yourself and your craft. In the event of a two-man upset, the men should swim on opposite sides of the capsized canoe.

Boarding an upright canoe full of water is not difficult. First, right it if it is capsized by reaching across to the far gunwale and rolling the canoe over. To board it, place your right hand over the far gunwale and left over the near one, press down on the canoe, and kick and swim your way over the canoe to a balanced position. Now roll over so that the back of your neck is on the far, and your legs over the near, gunwale and pivot to a sitting position. Try and keep as much of your body in the water all the time to increase balance and buoyancy. (Figure 32) If the canoe is not loaded too heavily, it will support up to three men hanging on its edge. Loaded with the usual equipment, it will easily float one man.

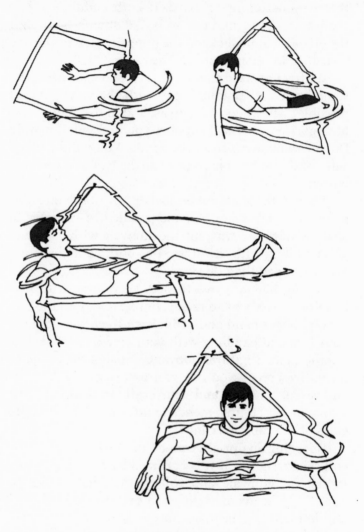

Figure 32
Self-Boarding (III)

Figure 33
The Shake-Out

If you are alone, you may need to empty the swamped canoe if it is far from shore. Lie low in the swamped canoe and kick and splash the water out. When most of the water has been removed in this fashion, the remainder can be bailed out with a boot or a hat.

A more efficient method of emptying a swamped canoe is the *shake-out*. (Figure 33) Roll the canoe over if it is upside down. Lean down hard at one end so that one end is completely under water and the other slightly elevated out of the water. Push hard, kicking back to get a good thrust, and about one-third of the water will flow out over the submerged end. Lift the submerged end quickly as soon as the water has stopped flowing out to prevent the canoe's refilling.

Repeat this action two or three times.

Now move to a position amidships and grasp the near gunwale with both hands. Depress the near gunwale almost to the water level and begin to shake out the water by rocking the canoe on its keel.

Kick hard to give yourself buoyancy so that your arms and shoulders are free to shake the canoe. Never rock the canoe over too far, because you will lose momentum if the far gunwale falls lower than the near one. Coordinate your breathing with the surge of the water so that you exhale as the water comes out over the gunwale (and into your face!). Rock the canoe in time to the water's surge to empty it completely and quickly.

Finally, board the canoe in the manner described above.

Regardless of the method you use to rescue yourself and your canoe, if there is another canoe near you when you upset, call (if there is not too much noise) or signal.

Rescue of Others

Although a canoe is not nearly as stable as a boat where rescuing others is concerned, it can be used for this purpose if the canoeist is careful to keep his canoe steady. In any case, rescue people first. Take care of the canoe and equipment later.

One obvious case for rescue is the capsized canoeist who is far from shore and tiring. Tell the swimmer to stay with the canoe and make your way over to it. If help is indicated, turn the canoe broadside to the swimmer, extend the paddle, and draw him in. When the swimmer is at the canoe, let him grasp the gunwale somewhat forward. Brace yourself and the canoe—by sitting in the bottom of the canoe and using a paddle brace—in case the swimmer panics and grabs at the canoe. It is best to tow the man in when the shore is close. But when the swimmer is exhausted and shore is distant, let him come aboard. Stabilize the canoe by sitting on the canoe bottom amidships, with both hands on the gunwales and feet against the sides of the canoe, and let the tired swimmer climb in over the edge. (Figure 34) There will be a sudden tilting of the canoe as he gets aboard, but you can counterbalance this movement by shifting your weight to one side or the other.

The capsized canoeist may be too tired to drag himself into your canoe, in which case you will have to stand up, balancing yourself carefully, and lift the victim up and out of the water into the canoe. (Figure 35) Needless to say, this maneuver requires a fine sense of balance, and it is essential that it be practiced many times before it is tried in a real emergency.

If you are unable to effect this rescue, you should

Figure 34
Rescue of a Tired Swimmer

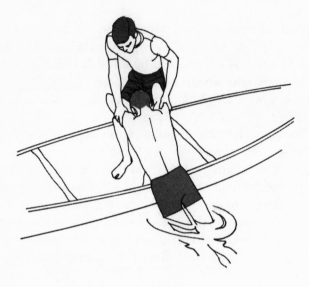

Figure 35
Rescue of an Exhausted Swimmer

lash the exhausted swimmer's wrists beneath a thwart, to prevent his drowning, and paddle quickly to the shore.

Alternatively, you can effect a *canoe-over-canoe rescue*. Once the canoeists are holding onto your canoe, you can empty and right theirs. Paddle alongside the capsized canoe. Roll it to an upside-down position. Then paddle to an end of the canoe, grasp the end, and lift it slowly up and over your canoe.

By the time the capsized canoe is balanced across yours, it will be empty, so roll it right-side up and slip it back into the water. The capsized paddlers can now board their own canoe again. (Figure 36)

To make it easier for them, however, paddle your canoe alongside theirs. Hold the two canoes together by grasping both gunwales, thereby providing stability while the capsized paddlers climb aboard.

Figure 36
Canoe-over-Canoe Rescue (I)

Figure 37
Canoe-over-Canoe Rescue (II)

If both canoes are capsized, you can still use the canoe-over-canoe method, by drawing one canoe over the keel of the other. Right one canoe and lift its end over the keel of the other. Then roll the lifted canoe over and draw it across the keel of the other. When the water has been emptied out, right the canoe and slide it off the keel, back into the water. (Figure 37) Board the righted canoe and use it to effect a canoe-over-canoe rescue of the canoe that remains capsized.

12

Clothing and Gear

It is essential to know the general climate of the country you're heading for if you are to choose comfortable, appropriate clothing. And clothing is one more thing that can decide the difference between a miserable experience and a pleasant, memorable trip.

There is no need to spend a lot of money on clothing. You can always use your regular outdoor garments, adding a sweater or extra shirt if the weather is on the cool side. Whatever the region, clothing must be sturdy and comfortable but not bulky. Take along what you will require—no more—and avoid extra weight. Almost anywhere you go canoeing in the summer the weather will be pleasant, so dress accordingly.

Keep your outfit light if you can. When in doubt as to camping clothing, look to either woolen or down-lined material. It will keep you warm when the weather turns rough, and when the weather becomes torrid, it can always be shed.

If you have to build up your wardrobe from scratch, be sure to take a look at the catalogues of companies that specialize in new outdoor equipment, from clothes and camping gear to preportioned, packaged meals. These catalogues make fascinating reading in themselves; the number of new time- and trouble-saving devices will amaze you. These products are often much lighter and less bulky, easier to maintain and use, more comfortable and even less expensive than traditional camping gear. Moreover, it is now possible to see and buy this new equipment in most large cities and outdoor-activities centers though the best-stocked outlets are still in Seattle, Washington; Portland, Oregon; Berkeley, California; and Denver and Boulder, Colorado.

Underwear

For an easy, one-week cruise, a suit of cotton underpants and undershirt may suffice. Cotton underwear is easily washed and dries out in no time. For a longer stay and for cooler weather, take along a suit of long underwear in the Duofold style, which is an undersuit of light wool with a cotton liner. The cotton next to the skin is smooth and soft, and the two layers of material trap air, giving ideal insulation: warmth without bulk. For cold weather, there is now available insulated underwear with nylon shell and acetate lining, which is also very comfortable for resting inside the tent or for wearing on a cold night. But the old favorite, wool, is still perfectly serviceable. Wool underwear will keep you warm until you can change even when it is wet.

Cotton underwear, ideal for the summer canoeist, takes on a clammy feel on wet, cold days, which are often encountered even in summer in the northern canoeing areas. If you do prefer cotton, therefore, the best solution is fishnet underwear, long popular in Scandinavia and now widely available in this country. Designed on the "air trap" principle, it's woven with knitted cells that hold the warm air against the skin, yet allow ventilation and prevent perspiration from forming.

Socks

For the summer camper a pair each of cotton and woolen socks will suffice. Socks can be laundered in no time (they feel best when they're clean). A pair of woolen socks is a great comfort when the weather is on the chilly side or during a rainy spell; wool is always more comfortable than cotton or synthetics when the feet are wet.

Trousers

Select camp trousers that can stand a lot of rough treatment. Almost every outdoorsman has an old pair he uses for hunting, fishing, or knockabout wear that will fill the bill. The trousers should be durable, with reinforced seams, turned-down cuffs, roomy pockets, and zippers that work. A loose-fitting pair of trousers will give you freedom in hiking and canoeing. Shorts are fine *in the canoe*. But around camp or on portages, you are likely to have your legs bitten and scratched if you wear shorts.

Shirting

Only one shirt is needed if you are traveling light. It should have a generous fit: roomy body, shoulders, and sleeves; a long tail that tucks in; long sleeves both to protect against the cold and the sun and to ward off insects; and two roomy breast pockets with flaps and buttons (pockets are essential on outdoor garments, especially on your shirt and jacket).

In the cooler climates the shirt should be wool. If the weather turns warm, the shirt can always be taken off. For warmer climates it may be of the increasingly popular synthetic fibers, excellent as shirting material, soft, pliable, and hard-wearing. In this category is the nylon "wind shirt" of lightweight fabric, which insulates the body in extra-cold conditions and can be worn either inside or outside other garments.

Sweaters and Jackets

The cool evenings and nights experienced much of the year in many parts of the country and in Canada mean that you should take along some top covering, and of course this is essential in cold weather. In summer, therefore, take along a light woolen sweater. In cold weather you may find a light sweater inadequate. At such times it is better to take two light sweaters rather than one heavy one, on the principle that warmth is a matter of insulation and not of weight, and that therefore two light sweaters will provide more warmth than one heavy one.

Jackets are acceptable in warm weather, but in cold weather they do not provide the protection and warmth that a sweater does, and should therefore not be taken.

Raingear

Always be prepared for the weather to turn wet and damp. Take along a lightweight raincoat. With a raincoat to shed the moisture and warm clothing underneath, you will be comfortable and able to enjoy your trip under all conditions.

Probably the best gear to have along in case of prolonged rain or drizzle—a situation bound to occur sooner or later—is a poncho that covers the whole body while you're paddling yet does not hamper your movement. The new ponchos made from lightweight coated nylon, with snaps to form sleeves and a drawstring hood, are the most practical and weigh only about 12 ounces. Vinyl plastic ponchos are very inexpensive. But while they will keep the rain out, they create perspiration problems and tend to snag and tear.

Instead of a raincoat or poncho you can use a parka, although it doesn't cover the legs. Probably no other item of clothing has seen so much improvement in the last few years as the parka. Now you can buy anything from a 4-pound down-filled oversize garment to a featherweight shell. A very convenient model is the nylon anorak, which weighs about 9 ounces. For intermittent summer rain, too, a good substitute is a jacket with a zipper. While zipper models let in cold air and are therefore not advisable in cold weather, in warmer weather the ease with which the zipper jacket can be put on and taken off is of great value.

Down clothing, although expensive, is a good investment if you're planning to spend prolonged periods in a cold climate. The insulation provided by goose down ensures comfortable temperature in both very cold and moderate weather. Down insulation is now available in parkas, vests, underwear, and even camping slippers.

Your hat or cap can be almost anything that is lying about in the closet. Where wet weather or hot sun is the prospect, I recommend a summer-weight hat *with a brim* to shade the eyes and part of the face and to keep water from trickling down your neck. If you're canoeing during the mosquito season, you can now get a nylon mosquito head net complete with metal supports that keep the net away from your face.

Footgear

Low-topped leather boots will be a fine choice for the canoe camper. They are light, sturdy, and, when chosen in a size that leaves room for two pairs of socks, very comfortable. Get a boot with eyelets instead of hooks and a rubber or composition sole. Make sure the boot does not rub at the heel.

To save on weight without sacrificing sturdiness, a good alternative is an imported rock-climbing shoe, the *kletterschuh*. This is a light and rugged suede boot with a leather inner lining and ridged rubber soles weighing only about 3 pounds per pair.

Boots with ridged soles will tend to carry dirt and leaves into the canoe, but they remain preferable to flat-soled boots because they more than compensate for the dirt with the grip they provide, especially in wet weather.

Avoid the so-called cowboy boots. They only invite sprained ankles, and their open tops make a handy receptacle for twigs and leaves, as well as for the rain that will just pour in.

Where the trip is sure to be a dry one throughout, or the canoe camper wants a light shoe for loafing around camp, the Indian-style moccasin is good. It also makes a good slipper when in the canoe. But a moccasin is undesirable in wet weather, for the leather becomes soaked in a jiffy and the soles become very slippery. Also, unless the camper has accustomed himself to this light, thin-soled shoe, he will develop sore feet in short order.

For the weekend jaunt tennis shoes are fine: light on the feet, easy to walk in, and inexpensive. And they grip rock well. They are especially good with two pairs of soft athletic socks to take the jar out of walking on rough terrain.

Rubber boots can be taken on the trip where much fishing is the prospect. But such footgear may often be unnecessary on the canoe cruise simply because in warm weather you can wade in the water with old boots or go barefooted. However, the camper-fisherman who plans a lot of stream fishing during his cruise will do well to include hip boots or waders.

Sleeping Gear

Many veteran canoe campers wear cold-weather clothing at all times, and for good reason. In many parts of the country even the hottest summer days are followed by bitterly cold nights. This is particularly true in the higher elevations and in the United States-Canadian border country, where there can be a difference of as much as 30–40 degrees between daytime and nighttime temperatures.

These conditions call for warm sleeping gear, which is best supplied by a down-filled sleeping bag. Choose a sleeping bag that is designed for cool weather and add a separate down liner as the weather gets colder. A liner allows the camper to adjust his warmth to the cold outside, either by using the liner as mattress and thereby adding to the insulation, or by sleeping between the layers of the liner. The liner should be exactly square so that it can be folded crosswise or lengthwise in the bag. It will help fill in the drafty gaps at the top of the bag and along the zipper side. In warm weather, of course, and when weight is a prime consideration, the liner can be eliminated.

Traditional sleeping bags are rectangular and have a canvas covering. Newer sleeping bags have a nylon shell and are much lighter as well as more comfortable and practical than the canvas ones; for instance, you don't have to fold them, you just stuff them pell-mell into a bag. They can be either rectangular or "mummy-shaped." According to U.S. Army data, in 40-degree weather you need 1½ inches of insulation; in 20-degree weather, 2 inches; in zero weather, 2½ inches; and at −20-degree weather, 3 inches. To get 2½ inches of insulation, you need a sleeping bag with about 2 pounds of down, giving an overall weight of about 4 pounds.

Along with the sleeping bag, include either a full-length or a three-quarter-length air mattress. I recommend the full-length size (32" x 74"), which offers comfort almost comparable with that provided by a modern innerspring mattress. A full-length air mattress weighs about 2½ pounds and folds into a small package. One of the best is the tufted airtight rubber mattress that is reinforced with a cloth covering. To save pack weight some campers prefer the three-quarter-length type. But most campers will find that for the comfort involved the full-length mattress is worth the slight additional weight.

A new substitute for the air mattress is the polyurethane foam pad covered in waterproof nylon. Although bulkier (but no heavier) than the air mattress, it provides more insulation and comfort, and it won't leak.

Equipment

The list of equipment and clothing below is intended as a guide only. You will have to make your own selection of equipment, based on such factors as the number of persons in the party, the length of the trip, the availability of stores en route, the time of the year, the weather expected, etc. It will always be possible to expand the list of "essentials" you "must" have with you, but all such extras will have to be paid for at every portage.

The inventive camper will use his ingenuity to make up for lack of equipment. For example, he will use a pointed stick and his ax or knife in place of a trenching tool. Yet at the same time he won't be afraid to include an item others may scoff at him for taking. If he must have something for his peace of mind, by all means he should take it along.

Suggested equipment and supplies for two persons:

1	Canoe
2	Paddles
2	Life jackets
1	Canoe and paddle repair kit
2	Packsacks and duffel bags
1	Tent
1	Groundsheet (or pack cloth)
2	Sleeping bags
2	Air mattresses or foam pads
1 set	Cooking and eating utensils
1	Primus stove and fuel
1	Folding bucket
2	Canteens
1	Can opener
1	Ax in sheath
1	Sheath knife
1	Jackknife
1	Folding saw
1	Sharpening stone
1	50' ⅜-inch line
1 box	Matches in waterproof container
6	Candles
1	Flashlight with extra bulb and batteries

1	First-aid kit, including snakebite kit
1 tin	Water-purifying tablets
1 pkg.	Bicarbonate of soda
1 can	Insect repellent
2	Toilet kits
2	Towels
1 pkg.	Detergent
1 roll	Toilet tissue
1 roll	Paper toweling
1 jar	Petroleum jelly
1	Sponge
1	Sewing kit
2 pr.	Sunglasses
2	Watches, pencils, notebooks
2	Compasses
	Maps of area
2	Whistles
2	Cameras, with extra rolls of film
	Fishing tackle
	Food (see Chapter 16)

Suggested clothing for one person:

1 pr.	Boots
1 pr.	Low shoes
1 pr.	Trousers
1 suit	Long underwear, two-piece
1 pr.	Woolen socks
1 pr.	Nylon socks
1	Long-sleeved woolen shirt
1	Nylon-cotton shirt
1	Insulated jacket
1	Felt hat with wide brim
1	Poncho or raincoat
1	Sweater
6	Handkerchiefs

A single-bit *ax* (about 27 inches long, with a

2-pound head) in a sheath is most commonly carried. But a smaller hatchet will do nicely where weight must be kept to a minimum.

Carry two *knives*. One should be a heavy jackknife with punch, screwdriver, and can opener, and one should be a short sheath knife, especially if there will be fish to clean and fillet. Carry a small whetstone for keeping the ax and knives sharp.

For camp lighting, candles have been the traditional standby. They are reliable, handy to use, and good fire starters in wet weather, so carry several. Candles can be used in candle lanterns that keep them from being snuffed out by the wind. The oldest type of lantern has a folding aluminum frame, but there are some very handy collapsible models made of light metal now on the market. If a lantern is not used, considerable care should be exercised to ensure that the candle does not set the tent interior or, worse, the occupants on fire.

Matches should be kept in a plastic box. You can even buy watertight survival kits containing waterproof and windproof matches that burn for half a minute in the highest winds. You can also buy "flint sticks," which need only be scraped with a knife to send off sparks. Or you can get tubes of hexamine, which, when spread on wood and lit, provides instant fire under the wettest conditions.

For illumination, the best thing is a small *flashlight* fitted with batteries bought fresh at the start of the trip. (Take along an extra bulb and batteries.) Choose a flashlight with a right-angle head that can be turned to focus anywhere inside the tent, or one of the various head lamps, used by miners and by Mt. Everest climbers alike, that leave both hands free. If you want the luxury of a well-lit campsite, then you should take along a kerosene lantern or one of the newer lanterns fueled by 6-hour cartridges.

13

The
Campsite

A camper can take a lot of punishment during the day if he knows that at the end of it he will get a substantial supper and a good night's rest. Both are essential, and both pretty well depend on picking the proper campsite.

Head for shore and make camp before the sun sets. It's a mistake to keep on paddling until you're exhausted or darkness has fallen. Start looking for a campsite while you're fresh and can still enjoy the evening around the campfire.

Pick your campsite carefully, with attention to such matters as wood and water supply, drainage, and favorable exposure. Seek a sheltered place, secure from wildlife.

If you can find a place near a spring, or a creek with spring water, you are in luck. In the wilderness regions one can dip drinking water right from the lake or river. But watch out for water pollution, a growing problem. If there is any question about water pollution, boil your water or use halazone tablets or iodine in the ratio of ten drops to a gallon of water, letting it set for fifteen minutes before drinking it.

To play it safe, take water with you and ration the supply. Plastic jugs or bottles are the best containers. If the canoe trip is a family outing, each child can have his own water canteen with his name taped on it to save time and argument.

You will need a supply of wood for the fire, and maybe for tent pegs and poles. Firewood may be a problem in some areas. Take advantage of such things as the deadwood left by beavers near their dams.

Check a possible campsite for good drainage. Not only is a high spot safe from rising water and heavy rains, but it will catch any cooling breezes blowing during the night. Well-drained ground is essential for a river camp because there is a chance the water may rise suddenly, especially during a rainstorm, and wash over the campground.

A high spot is good for another reason. Most canoe campers are summer vacationers and want no part of mosquitoes or other warm-weather insects. To avoid them when camping along a river or a lake, choose an open point where the wind can blow inshore and take the flies with it. If an open point is not available, select a high spot or a clearing.

Sandy soil close to a lake or stream is not recommended for a campsite. Not only is the ground too soft for holding the tent pegs, but sand flies and other insects seem to prefer the sandy areas near water, especially when the weather is warm.

Making Camp

You've picked your campsite, you're weary from a day of outdoor activity, and you're ready to set up camp for a good rest. Unload the canoes (remember to unload them while they're still floating free in the water) and pull them far enough up on shore so that they won't blow away if a storm arises. To be doubly sure, tie them down, too. Now pick out the best site for the tent. If you want to sleep warm and dry, set up your tent 10–15 feet above water level if it's possible. Dew or mist often rises high off water at night, and if your camp is enveloped in this moisture, you'll be anything but comfortable. Low ground has other disadvantages, too, such as night-long choruses of bullfrogs.

Don't set your tent up under big timber. Dead

branches are always breaking off large trees, especially in high winds. Then, too, during an electrical storm, large trees are apt to attract lightning.

Avoid game runways. Most animals are accustomed to using a certain run at night and will likely continue to use it—and if your tent is on that travelway, it might come to a sad end, along with the occupants.

There are several other precautions you can take against nosy wildlife. A manila or hemp rope laid around the campsite will often keep snakes out. Tying perishables up in a tree will thwart raccoons and bears.

Now that the tent site has been chosen, clear the ground of protrusions and set about erecting the shelter. As soon as the tent is up, the whole place takes on a warm, reassuring home-away-from-home atmosphere that presages a good night's sleep. Then select a place for the fire, a place to eat, and a place for the packs.

Each member should stake out a place to keep his gear, thus simplifying the camp routine. Take turns at the chores, with each member of the party pitching in and doing his assigned task. For example, one detail can square away the campsite, another can take care of the cooking, another bring firewood, another make the latrine and garbage pit. To build a latrine for the overnight camp, dig a saddle latrine 8 inches wide, 12 inches long, and 12 inches deep. After each use, throw in a spadeful of dirt. To build a garbage pit, dig a hole 12 inches in diameter and 12 inches deep.

"A place for everything and everything in its place," is a rule for a comfortable campsite; with this in mind and a work routine planned, making camp will go like clockwork. Before long the meal will be over, the tent up for the night, and your party sitting around the campfire enjoying the quiet evening.

There are few outdoor activities that challenge the ingenuity more than camp life. On the average "go-light" canoe cruise you may have little time or inclination to make a lot of fancy gadgets such as pot-hangers, brooms, cupboards, tables, chairs and the like. But when you are staying in camp for a couple of days there is always the desire to make camp life more enjoyable, as well as to keep busy, by fashioning certain conveniences. It is a chance to test your skill in woodcraft, making do with what you find in the forest.

Even when you are just staying overnight, most likely there will be time for repairing equipment, doing your washing, straightening out your pack, or cleaning up. There will be time for taking pictures, hunting, fishing, picking berries, or observing the animal and plant life around you. There is nothing more interesting than to spot a deer, a moose, an otter, a muskrat, or a mink, or to watch the antics of a loon or a flock of ducks on the lake when the day is done.

You have the whole of the great outdoors before you. The evenings can easily be made the most memorable part of the whole trip, times to look back on with pleasure when the trip is over.

14

Tents

Since camp on the canoe cruise is not only carried but shifted a lot as well, the best tent for the cruise is light and easily erected and dismantled. Poles and pegs should be kept to a minimum, especially when it will be possible to cut pegs right at the spot where the tent is to be erected.

The shelter must be compact. The material must be tough and waterproofed enough to shed rain well. The tent must roll up into a small bundle. Since the trip will often be through insect country, the shelter must be well screened and still have adequate ventilation.

This sounds like a big order, but such tents are readily available.

Materials

For the stationary camp the best material is usually waterproofed canvas or nylon. Some tents that fit the requirements have an external aluminum frame to do away with guy ropes and center poles. They are a bit bulky for the average canoe trip, however, unless the party is staying at one place for some time.

The nomadic tent that is light and compact suits most conditions. The simpler the tent for the "go-light" cruise, the better. What you want is a tent, large or small as the party requires, of a closely-woven, waterproofed, long-fibered cotton, or of durable nylon. Such a tent will come complete with lightweight aluminum poles, stakes, and guy lines in a carrying case, and will go up in minutes.

A steep roof is best for keeping dry in rainy weather. When erecting the tent, pitch and peg it so the material is smooth and taut to help turn rain away.

Tent Specifications

On trips with light packs, about 17 square feet of tent floor space per person should be allowed. Using this formula, tents in the 5-foot by 7-foot size are entirely suitable for two people, and tents of the 8-foot by 8-foot size, such as the miner's (discussed below), will accommodate three campers very nicely, and possibly four. However, when there are four or more campers, it is more satisfactory and healthy to use two small tents, such as two 5-foot by 7-foot tents, than one large tent.

A permanent sewed-in floor is definitely desirable. The tent with the sewed-in floor is compact, insect-proof, and quickly erected and dismantled.

Your tent should be adequately ventilated. Air should enter and circulate not only by the doorway but also by one or two vents in the tent. Some tents, such as the cruiser and crawl-in models, have a window set in the peak and covered with a hood, which shuts out the wind and rain but still permits air circulation.

Make sure there is nylon net in the door and vents, too, for keeping out small insects. (For the minute species, the "no-see-ums," there is very little you can do except carry a spray gun or "bomb" loaded with a powerful insect repellent and spray inside the tent before turning in for the night. These insect repellents cost only a little for the excellent job they do, often making the difference between a good night's rest and a bad one. However, do not spray directly on the tent fabric, because some sprays can destroy water repellency.)

Keep tent weight to a minimum. Even the tarp or pack cloth can be used as a tent. A spartan simplicity in shelters is the best idea. Improvise as you go along.

To recap: keep tent size, weight, ventilation, durability, and portability in mind when buying or renting a tent.

Popular Canoe-Camping Tents (Figure 38)

The Lean-To Tent. One of the perennial favorites with canoe campers, and of many a nomadic summer camper also, is the lean-to tent, especially the forester type. This shelter, about 8 feet deep and 6 feet wide at the front, slopes to a narrower width in the rear, where the occupants have their sleeping space. Two poles, making an inverted "V," support the tent at the front, and a ridge pole, fastened at one end to the point of the "V," slopes back and down.

The forester is light and practical, and excellent for two campers. It is designed so that heat from a fire built in front may be reflected into the interior, especially into the sleeping space. Held up by extra poles along the center ridge, it makes a good camp even for the snow season, when a sturdy ridge is needed for support. A mosquito screen usually covers the front or is draped over the sleeping area.

The forester tent affords a sturdy shelter with a minimum of time and trouble, provided it is pegged down firmly along the sides and back.

For the canoe camper who likes the open-front idea, there is another lean-to tent like the forester called the baker tent. For the spring or autumn camping trip it makes a warm shelter when the campfire is used for heat.

The baker is held up by four upright poles and a ridge pole. This tent slopes from the ridge pole to the rear, where there is a wall. A fly, attached to the front, can be extended to act as a canopy or dropped down and used as a wall, shutting off the tent. Its main advantage is its roominess, which makes for easy entrance and exit and gives space for movement. With the canopy down, it is insect-proof.

The Crawl-In Tent. An excellent summer tent for the canoe camper is the cruiser, also called the crawl-in. It is light and compact and has a sewed-in groundsheet, a vent at the rear ridge, a nylon-net front, and batwing flaps. With its porthole door, which can be shut off with flaps, and its 6-inch sill across the bottom, it can be made safe from rodents as well as snakes.

This little tent has a triangular tent flap that can be used as an awning. Measuring 5 feet by 7 feet in floor area and about 5 feet to the ridge line, it provides plenty of room for two people and their gear. The cruiser is bug-proof and is especially popular in the mosquito-plagued areas of Canada, Alaska, and the northern United States. It is a good trail tent almost anywhere.

The Pup Tent. The pup tent is wedge-shaped, easily packed, easily erected, and, in a 5-foot by 7-foot size, large enough for two people. Fitted with a sewed-in groundsheet, it makes ideal sleeping quarters where weight is of primary concern. It goes up or down in minutes and by its very simplicity has endeared itself to backpackers for years.

The Two-Man "High-Lite" Tent. Another wedge-shaped tent, somewhat on the order of the pup tent, is the High-Lite. This tent is light: complete with stakes, poles, and guy lines, it weighs only 57 ounces. It is made of densely-woven nylon and has a storm door that can be staked out as windbreak when you want to cook.

In the two-man style, the floor length of the Hi-Lite is 7 feet, floor width 5 feet at the front, tapering to 4 feet in the rear. The height at the front is 4 feet, and the rear-wall height is 2 feet. It has a sewed-in floor of waterproof nylon, a very good feature for any trail tent.

Featherweight tents of tightly-woven synthetic fabrics, such as this one, make good portable shelters even in cold regions. Nylon and Dacron tents are more durable and lighter than those made of cotton, but they do have poor breathing qualities. Fitted with vents, and with the doorways open, however, there is usually enough air for sleeping.

The Miner's Tent. The closed, tepee-type tent, such as the miner's, which turns away insects and weathers well, meets possibly 90 per cent of the requirements for outdoor shelters.

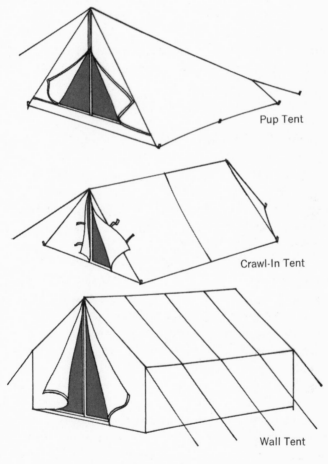

Figure 38
Types of Tent

The miner's, or pyramid, or plainsman's, tent, whichever you call it, is simple in construction, easily erected, and easy to carry. A center pole some 6 feet high holds it up, allowing standing room inside, and there are no guy ropes to fuss with. It has the advantage of a steep roof for shedding rain.

Another feature of the miner's is that the flaps at the front not only open up from top to bottom to allow the shelter to be heated by a fire but usually can also be tied out on both sides to break the wind and provide a space for cooking.

For its very simplicity this type of tent is a fine choice for the canoe camper. Erecting and dismantling is no chore, and the tent itself is light and durable and capable of standing up in stiff winds when well staked out.

For two or three campers, a good size for this tent is 8 foot by 8 foot; in this size it weighs about 7 pounds in a lightweight waterproof cotton. It weighs less in nylon, of course.

The Wall Tent. One more tent to be considered is the wall tent. It is higher and longer at the ridge than most trail tents, the roof slants gradually, and the tent has upright walls—all of which place it in high favor with campers who want more living room and wish to move in and out with ease. For the cold-weather camper who wants to shut his tent off and heat it with an inside stove, the wall tent is especially suitable.

The wall tent has good headroom. The sidewalls allow room for air circulation and easy moving about, and even the use of cots. It can withstand high winds and heavy rains when well rigged out. For family camping, especially when taking it easy around a lake or stream, this tent is well worth considering.

15

A Campfire
in Any Weather

A campfire is a definite asset to the canoe cruise. In wet weather this is especially so. While charcoal and Sterno and other such materials are increasingly used for the sake of ease and convenience, it is a campfire, more than anything, that offers good cheer and comfort in the evening. Moreover, you can start and keep a good blaze going in almost any weather by following simple rules, with here and there a little trick or two.

Remember to take along stick matches to light your fire or stove. Carry them in a fireproof and waterproof container, a plastic bottle being the most convenient. The matches can't ignite themselves accidentally by friction, and if the canoe should overturn, the bottle will float and keep the matches dry. Or use flint sticks to get sparks.

Campfire in Dry Weather

In dry weather obtain a permit for an open fire from game or fire wardens if there are signs or warnings in your area indicating that this is necessary. If the fire is permitted, take proper precautions to pick an open spot, preferably near water, and never build the fire under overhanging branches.

At a spot some distance from where the tent will stand, scrape away all flammable material until the bare ground is reached and build your fire here. Steer clear of areas where evergreens have formed a heavy bed of needles on the forest floor and of peaty ground, dry musk, moss, and lichens, for these materials are quite flammable and may flare up quickly when struck by a spark. I recall one time moving into a campsite in northern Michigan where smoke was rising some fifty feet from the original fireplace, having burned underground for days.

For kindling use the softwoods, such as cedar, balsam, spruce, tamarack, and pine. Split the kindling fine for a starter and use bark and dry twigs to get a sharp, quick blaze. Dead twigs at the base of trees, if snap-dry, are excellent kindling. When you have a good fire going, begin to pile on large pieces of wood. You need draft always, even in dry weather. So don't put on too much wood at once. Avoid wood that has lain flat on the ground for some time; it is usually rotten. And remember: wherever you are, don't cut down living trees.

Confine your fire. Line the spot with rocks, or if there are no rocks, build it in a shallow hole or trench or remove the turf and use the pieces to provide a fire wall. A fireplace lined with rocks often will suffice to keep the fire in bounds, but in extremely windy weather or when the woods are very dry, dig a trench for the fire. The wind will have a tendency to sweep over it, and sparks will be kept down.

Never leave a fire untended. Keep a pail of water or a bucket of sand handy to douse the fire in case it starts to spread. Never leave a fire to burn itself out. Instead, when you're ready to leave, douse the fire with water or dirt, or both, making sure that it is not burning underground. Too many forest fires have been started by careless campers. By taking a few necessary precautions with the campfire, the woods can be kept safe for man and wildlife.

Fire in Wet Weather

Start with the kindling. When it's raining, you will have to go to some pains to get dry wood, and it is a good plan to carry twigs from one campsite to the next if rain threatens. Split the kindling into thin slivers so it will catch fire readily. Look for the obvious sources of dry wood: fallen branches or a dry deadfall, either a tree or stump. Don't chop down trees. It is poor conservation; moreover, most live trees don't burn well. There are all too many dead trees lying around just waiting to be reduced to kindling.

If the ground is wet, build the fire on a platform of wood chunks laid crosswise, with space for draft left between them, or on flat rocks. The elevation provides a good supply of oxygen as well as insulation from the wet ground.

Set kindling in a pyramid or lay it crosswise and start the fire at the base of the pile. Use dry bark or paper for lighting, and when the wood begins to blaze, add small pieces of dry splinters or shavings to interstices, nursing the fire along until it becomes a steady blaze. (Figure 39)

You must have draft. Don't pile on too much firewood at the outset, especially if it is a bit wet. Get a good fire going with the kindling, then add the firewood sparingly. Once the fire is blazing well, you can add more wood, especially when you want to dry out. And drying out is the first requirement. You need heat and flames for this; the hot coals needed for cooking can come later.

Hardwoods Are Best Fuel

Every locality varies in its supply of kindling and firewood, but usually the ridges and high ground offer the best fuel. Unless you have no choice, bypass such trees as alder, willow, elm, and other softwoods growing in marshes and river bottoms. What the camper wants for firewood, if he has the choice, are hardwoods: hickory, oak, beech, ash, birch, ironwood, poplar, and maple. These woods may be hard to cut, especially with a hand ax, and thus the small folding saw will prove very valuable, but they will burn longer and emit stronger and more even heat than the softer woods. Also, the hardwoods burn down to a bed of fine cooking embers instead of turning to ashes quickly as the softwoods do.

Ready to Cook

When the fire has died down a little, scrape it together and then feed it small sticks of dry wood as needed, confining the blaze to the underside of the kettles or pans you're using for cooking. Now you're set to heat a kettle for coffee or tea for that lovely feeling of warmth and security. If you've brought a grid, heat the kettle on that. If you don't have a grid, you can easily rig up a pole to hang the kettle over the fire. Find a sapling pole with a forked end and cut a length about 6 feet long. If the cutting has no forked end, cut a notch in it over which to slip the kettle bail. Sharpen the thicker end and drive it into the ground, slanting it over the fire slightly and propping it up at the desired angle with a log or rocks or another forked stick.

Figure 39
Setting a Campfire

By the time the water or coffee is boiling, the fire will probably have burned down to hot embers, and then it's time for the frying pan. A hot bed of coals makes an ideal cooking fire, whereas a blaze would likely set the grease on fire or otherwise cause trouble.

The trench fire will probably provide the best cooking fire, because in it the heat will be concentrated. Such a fire is especially good for meals that require a long period to cook. As a rule, a little fire goes a long way for cooking if it is kept confined to a small space and hardwood is used for fuel.

Making a Cooking Range

If you intend to cook several meals at the campsite, the single propped stick might not suffice, and then a more permanent crane should be made. The framework is merely two forked sticks, about 2 feet high, driven upright into the ground about 5 feet apart, and a thick green sapling pole laid on them horizontally over the fire.

Figure 40
Campfire Cooking Range

To make pothooks for this cross-pole, cut two or three green forked sticks of varied lengths and at the end of one arm of each cut a deep notch. Invert the forked sticks on the cross-pole and over the fire and hang the kettles on the notch. Use the longer crotches for quick heat and the shorter for slow heat or for simmering.

To complete the cooking range, cut and haul to the fireplace two logs each about 3 feet long. Bed them in the ground to form a "V," leaving the flattest part exposed on top, so that the fire can be built between them. Then use the flat tops as counters on which to lay the pots and pans for close-to-the-fire cooking.

With the crane, kettle holders, and flattened logs, the camper has a cooking range made to order—and all gotten right in the vicinity. (Figure 40)

Backlog Fire

In the cold of the night the camper might want a fireback, or backlog, fire to reflect heat into the tent. Such a fire will burn for some time without being replenished and will radiate much heat. (Figure 41)

To construct a solid fireback arrangement, cut down a green sapling about 3 inches in diameter. From this sapling cut two stakes 3½ feet long, sharpen the butt end of each, and drive them at an acute angle, with the slope away from the tent, into the ground, parallel to the tent front and about 6 feet from it. The stakes should be about 2½ feet apart. Cut logs to lie against these stakes, and set them firmly one on top of the other to the height of the stakes. Now light the fire against this fireback.

After the fire has gained strength, add heavier logs of green hardwood until it's blazing well. If the fireback logs making up the framework of the fireback are green and quite thick, they will last several nights before burning through. The camper may have to replenish the fuel supply during the night, but with this little care the fireback will radiate much heat

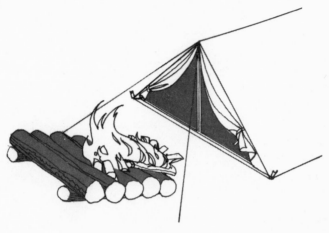

Figure 41
Backlog Fire

with a minimum of upkeep. During the spring and fall months, the canoe camper who has no time or space for a stove will find this type of fire a boon, and often it will make the difference between a good and a bad night's sleep. The camper will find he is well repaid for the little time he spent making his fire.

16

Tips on Wilderness Cooking

There is no sweeter sound than the sizzle of bacon frying over the coals, no better aroma than arises from the campfire at mealtime. Even the most inexperienced cook won't find it hard to whip up a meal over an open fire, if he goes about it with a little imagination, ingenuity, and common sense.

Simple Dishes

Plain dishes are your best bet for camp cuisine. They satisfy outdoor appetites and are easy to prepare. Avoid complicated recipes; the fewer the ingredients and procedures, the easier the cooking will be. Make your meals simple: vegetables can be boiled or baked; meat can be broiled, fried, or stewed. It is easier to keep your larder to staples.

Measurements often worry the amateur cook unduly. A little too much of this or too little of that will not make much difference in the eating; except for seasonings and baking powder, proportions of ingredients are not a critical matter. If there is any doubt about how much salt or pepper to use, lean toward the light side and let the other campers add more if they desire. In the case of baking powder, it is better to use plenty rather than little so that the biscuits will be sure to rise and come out light and fluffy.

Why Do It the Hard Way?

The camp cook has a friend in the prepared mixes that are now readily available for breads, rolls, cakes, soups, and desserts. In a prepared biscuit mix, for instance, the cook gets not only the baking powder but almost all the ingredients right out of the box. Of course, these mixes don't equal the home-cooked product, but they will do in a pinch and they help make camp cooking easy as well as varied.

The freeze-dry process of preserving and dehydrating also now makes it possible to carry along a package containing two boneless pork chops, mashed potatoes with gravy, whole-kernel corn—all quite tasty, enough for two persons—weighing only 7 ounces. Trail packets for four persons, which need only the addition of water and a few minutes' cooking, are available in a great variety of foods—from chicken à la king (8 ounces) to chocolate cream dessert (5 ounces). These are very inexpensive and can be stored for long periods without deteriorating. Then, too, cooking is made easy by the use of aluminum foil. If food-portions are prepacked in foil, they can be taken out of the food sack and cooked without further ado. But even without this initial preparation, wrapping food in foil makes cooking easy, quick, and clean.

When Is the Food Done?

You can tell when the food is done over the campfire just as you can in the kitchen. Boiled or baked vegetables and meat are done when they can be pierced easily with a fork. Boiled potatoes may take some time to cook, but you can shorten their cooking time by cutting them into smaller pieces. They're done when they're mealy and soft. Cook beans, rice, and hot breakfast cereals over a low fire. Most hot cereals come precooked and take little time to prepare.

Bread or cake is done when you can pierce it with

a sliver of wood and the wood comes out clean. Fish is done when a fork prod tells you that it's flaky.

Cooking Utensils

Assemble a cooking kit that fits the kind of cooking you'll be doing on the trail. Aluminum or tinned steel is customary; a set of seamless aluminum vessels is best because it's light and won't crack (enamelware will). Get pots and pans that nest into each other; all the cooking utensils should fit into the largest kettle you're taking. Keep the whole package in a waterproof bag.

Pots and other utensils should have folding, removable handles for compactness. Take along wire bails so pots can be hung over the campfire and pot covers to keep out flying ashes, insects, and the like.

A party of four will need one coffeepot, two frying pans, one bucket, two stew pots, and one or two removable handles. The whole outfit should fit into the largest vessel and weigh no more than 4 pounds.

For cups and plates, plastic is better than aluminum. Plastic can be held in the hand no matter how hot the food or beverage, and it doesn't let things cool off so fast. You will need a plastic cup and plate for each member of your party. Choose plates of thick, tough plastic with deep sides so that they can be used for soups and stews as well as bread and meat.

Along with these things, carry silverware in a plastic or cotton bag. For a party of four, carry four each of knives, forks, and tablespoons. Also take along a can opener and a butcher knife. Other handy utensils are a pancake turner (with wooden handle), a large cooking spoon, and salt and pepper shakers.

Plastic cups with partial handles—that is, with handles that have a gap between cup and handle at the bottom—that nest into each other are recommended. Cups are all-purpose vessels—good for coffee, soups, and even main dishes—so you may want to double the number of cups.

Make sure your frying pan is heavy; a thin pan will warp badly and cannot be used for pan broiling since food will adhere to it. "Teflon" pans make admirable utensils for the camp cook for this reason.

If your pans are not equipped with handles at the outset and you forget to take along handles for them, it is easy to fashion short wooden handles for them, wooden inserts being better than metal since they do not get too hot.

Portable Stove

A real boon for the roving camper, when it can be handled easily, is the small, portable Primus stove. A common make weighs only 6 ounces; it is safe, light, and compact and burns for 90 minutes on 8 ounces of white gas, naphtha, or Coleman fuel. It is self-priming and fast-starting. A portable stove is not a necessity on the trail, but there are many times—for instance, when the weather is cold and nasty—when it is worth its weight in gold.

Folding Reflector Oven

One item worth considering is a folding reflector oven, to be used for baking biscuits, bread, etc., and for roasting. Such a collapsible reflector baker, carried in a waterproof bag, will be appreciated by the camper who wants a varied diet.

This oven can be used either with an open fire or with a camp stove. Many foods, such as biscuits, bread, johnnycake, baked beans, and other hot dishes, can be turned out very tastily with an oven. Some experimentation must be undertaken to find out just how much heat is required for baking with this oven, but success is no great trick with it.

An aluminum oven accommodating a 10-inch by 12-inch pan weighs about 2 pounds. It should be kept polished for best results, since the baking is affected by the heat reflected from above and below the oven. Place the oven to the windward side of the fire to prevent ashes from blowing on the food. Set it about 12 inches from the fire at first, and after that determine the proper distance by the heat of the fire and the speed of baking. A lively fire, not too high, is best when using the oven.

What Goes in Your Food Pack?

Make a checklist for food, so you don't find yourself miles from nowhere minus some such necessity as salt, sugar, butter, or coffee. The food pack listed below contains a combination of staples, specialized items, and fresh, dried, and canned foods, enough for 2 persons on a 10-day trip. It will weigh, at the beginning of the trip, about 60 pounds. Your personal preferences, and those of your family or party, will guide you in making substitutions or additions to the list.

Meats and Fats

2 lbs.	Fresh meat
5 lbs.	Slab bacon
6 lbs.	Ready-to-eat ham
1 lb.	Shortening
2 lbs.	Butter
2 lbs.	Salami
2 lbs.	Cheese
3 cans	Corned beef
2 pkgs.	Hot dogs

Breadstuffs

3 loaves	Wrapped bread
2 pkgs.	Instant cereal
4 lbs.	Pancake flour
3 lbs.	Biscuit powder
¼ lb.	Baking powder

Dry-Pack Foods

2 lbs.	Powdered milk
3 lbs.	Instant potatoes
½ lb.	Dried onions
¼ lb.	Dried carrots
¼ lb.	Dried corn
¼ lb.	Dried peas
¼ lb.	Dried eggs
¼ lb.	Dried yams
4 pkgs.	Dried soups
8 2-man	Freeze-dried dinners

Beverages

3 lbs.	Coffee
16	Tea bags
½ lb.	Cocoa

Sweets

5 lbs.	Sugar
1 lb.	Powdered orange drink
4 lbs.	Dried fruit
3 pkgs.	Instant pudding mix
1 lb.	Jam or jelly
3 lbs.	Chocolate bars

Miscellaneous

½ lb.	Salt
1 can	Pepper
2 jars	Peanut butter
1 jar	Jam
1 bottle	Pickles
1 bottle	Catsup

1 bottle	Syrup
4 cans	Pork and beans
1 lb.	Whole onions
3 large cans	Evaporated milk
1 jar	Mustard
1 doz.	Eggs

Notes on Foods

Keep food dry. Items that can melt or spread and be messy, such as jelly, butter, bacon grease, should go in cans with screw-on lids—never in plastic containers, which absorb and hold food odors. Put dry foods in polyurethane bags and keep these in turn in cloth bags with tie strings. Carry all the food in a waterproof packsack.

Keep foods out of reach of all animals. Use leftovers for snacks the following day. Vary your diet with the foods nature provides—fish, berries in season, fruits, nuts—but be sure you know which are edible.

Snacks

Sometimes it may be inconvenient to stop for lunch, or you might decide to postpone eating for a few hours, because of rain or because you want to make it to a certain campsite by nightfall. It is then good to have handy some quick-energy food to munch while paddling. A favorite of sportsmen is a 4–5-ounce pack of chocolate chips, raisins, and other dried fruits such as figs, which you can prepare in advance in a plastic bag and slip inside a pocket in the morning. A few nibbles of such a mixture are enough to keep you going in an emergency for a long time. Then, too, you can now buy candy bars especially designed to provide maximum energy in a minimum of time. In fact, any food with a high sugar content will replenish lost energy very quickly, and some should be carried for emergencies.

Clean-Up

Clean up around camp right after each meal. Set a kettle of water to heat over the fire. Meanwhile, wipe dishes clean with grass or leaves—which you should then burn in the campfire. Scrub dirty pots with sand. Use a liquid detergent. Rinse the dishes in hot water. Pour the dirty dish water into a small rock-filled hole dug in the ground. Burn all litter from the meal—wrappers, papers, napkins, table scraps, aluminum foil, and tin cans. Burned cans and foil should be crushed and buried along with any empty glass jars or bottles. Keep your campsite neat and clean at all times, for your own sake and for those who will follow you.

On weekend trips in heavily traveled areas take along heavy-duty plastic bags in which to take out garbage. Too many persons digging garbage pits or burning refuse in fire pits at a favorite stopping point can quickly spoil the attractiveness of the area. *Conservation-minded outdoorsmen carry out what they carry in wherever possible.*

17

How to Beat
the Insect Problem

Early in spring and late in fall the canoe camper will have little trouble with insects. In summer it is another matter. Then, wherever the canoeist travels, he will no doubt meet with some kind of bothersome insects. How he will fare is pretty much a matter of preparation.

Insects are either biters or stingers. The biters are mosquitoes, "no-see-ums," several species of flies, chiggers, ticks, and spiders; the stingers are wasps, hornets, bees, and scorpions. (Figure 42)

The biggest pest is the common *mosquito,* especially prevalent in swamps and marshy places. Sun and strong wind are hard on this pest and are therefore conditions to seek when picking a campsite in the summer. Netting and screening and spray-on insect repellent will protect you from mosquitoes inside a tent. When you're in the mosquitoes' favorite grounds, spray yourself liberally with a mosquito repellent. Then if you do get bitten, apply "anti-sting" medicine at once.

Of a more vicious and hardy breed than the mosquito is the *blackfly* (or buffalo gnat, as it is also called because of its humped back). This fly is smaller than a housefly, black, fast-moving, hardworking, gregarious, and it is a fierce biter. It is found mostly in mountainous regions and in the land of the northern conifer, such as the Great Lakes states and Canada. One consolation about this fly is that, like the mosquito, only the female bites; another is that the fly is prevalent mostly during only two months, June and July. I know many avid outdoorsmen who will not venture into the woods during these two months because of this pest.

If you run into a swarm of blackflies, you'll have a job getting rid of them. The blackfly attacks en masse, madly, doing its best to get under your clothing. It will dig in along the collar, hairline, wrists, and ankles —any place where the skin is exposed and it has a chance to crawl inside the clothing.

The best way to beat this fly is to keep in the open as much as you can, since it dislikes any kind of breeze.

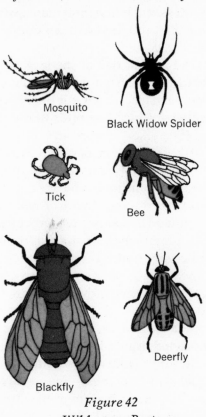

Figure 42
Wilderness Pests

When a horde does attack, just leave the premises; you'll never win unless you can kill them all.

It's said that this black pest can kill cows, horses, and game animals, and from one memorable encounter with this devastating fly I fully believe it. The time was June, the place was the Big Presque Isle River in northern Michigan. We were after trout, and while our fishing party was in the open, we hardly knew there were flies around. But when we got into the brush and trees around our trout stream, the blackflies almost murdered us.

We were well dressed for the occasion, but that seemed to make little difference to these flies. They descended in millions, swarmed all over us, bit bloody welts into our faces and hands, and managed to get not only under our shirt collars but under our hats and up our sleeves.

On that trip I caught one of the largest trout I've ever taken, but I paid dearly for it. When my partners and I somehow managed to get out of the woods, our faces were welters of bleeding bites that did not heal for days.

Another little flying pest, one that is much more common than the blackfly, is the "no-see-um," a biting gnat or midge that can hardly be seen even when it alights but that has a painful way of boring into the skin. Also called sand fly, punky, and creeping fire, this small gnat can seemingly burn its way into exposed skins. It can be very bothersome, especially when it descends in swarms, as is its usual procedure.

Found near water, this midge is most active in the morning and evening. An insect repellent will keep this minute pest at a distance, but if there are too many in the neighborhood, leave.

If you must put up with this ubiquitous little pest —say, after the tent is erected—make sure that the netting is secure, spray the tent well with a strong repellent, and then get inside. Chances are that by the time you're ready to retire for the night, the midges will have vanished. If they haven't, give them another dose of the spray.

Another pair of winged pests, found mostly in the mountainous and coniferous country, are *deerflies* and *moose flies*. These two-winged devils, the black and yellow deerfly and the purple-black, brown-winged moose fly, come around mostly when the weather is warm and sunny, and when they can detect the odor of perspiration from the active outdoorsman. They have an uncanny way of finding people, and when they do, they will stick on the trail until they or their intended victims win out.

Unlike the blackflies, the deerflies and moose flies rarely travel in swarms. But when one or two do spot a likely victim, they buzz around, dodging and darting about until they finally find an opening. Then they bore in like a bullet. They go for the face, the neck, the hands, and if a man is not wearing a hat, they will zero in for the hair. This fly can be handled only one way: wait for it to land and then smash it. But you will have to anticipate the attack and get the fly almost before it alights because it is on target immediately, biting as it lands.

Deerflies and moose flies are not too common in most camping areas, but if they are around, they will make their presence known, usually on a sunny day and before sundown. This fly can be kept out of your tent with bobbinetting; it is when you are casually carrying on your outdoor activities that the deerfly and the moose fly will get in their licks. So wear a hat, strike back fast when you see one hovering about, and you may escape unscathed.

Other camping pests are *ticks* and *chiggers*, found mostly in the South and Southwest and along the eastern coast. The tick is the more widespread of the two. A non-flyer, it will attach itself to a person as he brushes against foliage and either bore into the skin at or near the place it alights or crawl well down inside the clothing and make itself at home. The tick digs in with its head, sucking blood, inducing a sore and swollen spot. The victim is sometimes able to feel the tick crawling around and can then get rid of it. But very often it will dig in and bury its head in the skin before it is discovered.

To rid yourself of one of these little diggers, apply a drop of kerosene, alcohol, gasoline, or grease to it to cut off its air supply. A quicker way is to touch the tick with a lighted match or cigarette. Given this "hot-foot," the tick will pull out fast. However, if it is embedded too deeply, it must be removed from the skin with tweezers. Make sure you lift it out very carefully so that all of the bug is removed; otherwise, the remains will fester. Since a tick can carry disease, it must be dealt with quickly and cleanly. After removing it, wash the bite with soap and water or treat it with a strong antiseptic. It is wise to check the inside of your clothing and your bare hide at the end of the day for the presence of this bothersome insect.

A chigger is an extremely small insect with a sharp, nasty bite. Especially irritating is the itching that results from its bites and often lasts for days. Scratching can lead to infection, so this insect should be avoided if possible. A good application of insect repellent to the body should deter this pest.

In some parts of the country the camper may also run into *spiders*. The most dangerous are the black widow, the tarantula, and the newly discovered brown recluse spider. The bite of any of these spiders is very painful and, in the case of the black widow and the brown recluse, can be fatal, especially for a child or an elderly person.

These spiders are distinctive in appearance and can usually be spotted before they do any damage, so you should learn to identify them. The black widow is a medium-sized, shiny black spider with an orange mark on its abdomen in the shape of an hourglass. It is found mainly in the southern part of the United

States; few have penetrated far into the North. The tarantula is a fierce-looking spider, 2 inches long with a 4–5-inch leg spread; it is found mostly in the Southwest. The brown recluse is about ½ inch long and has only 6 legs. It has a violin-shaped marking on its back and is any color between light yellow and dark brown. Discovered only a few years ago, in southern Illinois, it is now spreading northward.

If they are to be found in the country you're heading for, learn to identify these and other potential pests before leaving on your camping trip. If children are going on the trip, make sure they can recognize these spiders and other dangerous pests such as snakes and the stinging insects.

In the stinger category there are wasps, hornets, bees, and scorpions. *Wasps,* which like to nest on low-hanging branches, will rarely sting unless disturbed, so it pays to watch for and avoid them. *Bees* and *yellow jackets* build their nests in the ground or on logs and hollow trees. When you spot a nest, walk—don't run—away from it. Hasty movements will only attract the stingers, so move away slowly. *Scorpions* are found mostly in the Southwest. Be especially careful to examine boots and shoes and other such items into which scorpions could get in the night—before you put them on.

To be one up on these and other flying insects, dress defensively in long-sleeved and long-legged garments and use insect repellents and a sharp eye.

Despite all precautions, you will probably be bitten by a mosquito or a gnat, at least, but a few good "anti-sting" medicines should get you by with little discomfort. An alcohol wash is effective, as are applications of ice, cold water, or cold mud (the last, especially, when stung by a bee or wasp). Washing with a strong hand soap is good; a paste of sodium bicarbonate is very effective.

Insects are becoming less trouble as more campers

arm themselves with repellents, spray guns, and insect bombs. Thus armed, the canoe camper can strike out anywhere, anticipating a relatively pest-free time.

Just for safety, keep a snakebite kit on hand. Read the instructions carefully before your trip so that you will be able to use it immediately if necessary, and make yourself familiar with types of *snakes* to be found in the area you are going to visit, and with the specific treatment for each type of snakebite.

The first thing to do if someone in your party is bitten is to keep him lying down and as quiet as possible. Excitement and exertion increase the blood circulation and add to the danger. Tie a handkerchief or bandage of some kind firmly above the wound to slow down the flow of blood and keep the poison from spreading. Do not tie the tourniquet too tightly, however, nor keep it on too long—remove it for about one out of every fifteen minutes.

Make diagonal incisions about ¼ inch long through the punctures with a sterilized knife or a razor blade, using extreme care not to cut into major tendons or blood vessels. Then suck out as much poison as possible with a suction cup, or with the mouth, if there is no open sore in the mouth. Continue with suction for half an hour unless a doctor can take over sooner.

Get the patient to a doctor as soon as possible. If a trip is necessary, move him as quietly and gently as possible.

It is best to avoid those areas where poisonous snakes are a menace; an ounce of prevention here is certainly worth a pound of cure. On the other hand, few snakebites are deadly, unless the victim is a small child or a weak adult.

18

Play It
Safe

Before setting out on its cruise, the canoe party should inform some responsible person, or some agency near the takeoff point, of the details of the proposed trip. Write down the place of departure, proposed route, expected time of arrival at destination, and the names and addresses of the members of the party and of persons to be contacted in an emergency. Keep a copy on your person so that the details given will not be forgotten.

Don't take chances. Better to make it a relaxed trip than an ambitious project that involves needless risks. You'll probably be a long way from a doctor, so preventing accidents is very important. Be careful when handling the ax. Use a long-handled ax and kneel down when chopping and splitting wood. Never hold the wood chunk in one hand and split it with the other.

Watch your step, especially on the portages. Many such trails are rocky, and a fall with a heavy pack could result in serious injury. On the first trip along an unfamiliar portage carry the lightest gear first, improve the trail if it needs it, and avoid straining at all times.

Finding the Way

Each member of the canoe party should carry, and know how to use, a compass. The seasoned canoe camper uses his compass much of the time when traveling in unfamiliar areas. He wants to know where he is and where he is going, so he keeps the compass in an accessible place and uses it. When he correlates its use with a study of the map he is carrying (and always carries), he will be able to determine his whereabouts pretty closely.

Good maps of the region you plan to travel are easily obtained unless the area is exceptionally remote. A map scale of 1 inch to 1 mile is best. Just how well you use the map may be the difference between having difficulty with directions and routes and finding your way along the course smoothly, with little lost time.

When heading into strange country, fix your position and the main features of the region in mind before you even drop the canoe in the water. Every evening, too, you should know how many miles you will have to travel along this waterway before you reach a point of debarkation. What general direction will you be traveling? Are there portages along the way? Just where are they? How long? Are they marked? And how do you go about finding the right trail and keeping it once you find the portage entrance?

Are there hills or other prominent features of the landscape to guide you as you paddle along? Can you find your way back again by the same route? Which direction do you take when you find yourself in a big lake with a lot of islands, one looking pretty much like another? Do they show on the map? Can you steer a clear course where the lake widens out? Just where is the mouth of the next river you are heading for?

Don't get lost or mixed up in your directions. The experienced canoeist takes pains to know the nature of the waters he will encounter. On the trip he is guided by such things as wind direction, position of the sun, natural landmarks, hills and valleys, trees, points of land, trails, portages, drainage, and many other characteristics of the region, which he is careful to note on maps beforehand and to observe as he travels along, both on land and on water.

Study your route and make sure of it by checking your map, taking your compass bearings, and making mental notes of the lay of the land. Perhaps you want to return the way you've come. In that case, mark your route by noting landmarks that have meaning for you; mark the trail with blazes. The main thing is to know where you are and how to get back with no trouble.

It pays to ask directions—a lot of them—before departure. Your canoe outfitter and other canoe travelers no doubt have made this trip and can point out landmarks and pencil in your route on a detailed map of the area. These experienced canoe campers can also note the mileage between certain important points and fill you in on the outstanding features of the region and route.

There may be one man in your party who has a flair for map reading and finding the way; let him be the navigator. When in doubt, let the most capable woodsman plot the course and explain to the party from time to time just where they are and where they are going. Another man should keep a daily journal of the trip. Not only will the journal help if you get lost, but it will also provide a fascinating account of the trip when you return home.

No member of the party should stray far from the canoe and the outfit, the source of substance and equipment. Stay together at all times and never part with any of the gear.

Tips for the Novice

But what to do if you're green in the woods? Canoe campers and cruisers are not all cut from the same mold, seasoned and hardened in the ways of the wilds. If the man who plans his route and checks the trail and compass can be temporarily "confused" at times, what might happen to you if you are young and lack experience? How can you anticipate trouble?

In the first place employ a guide—the first time

out, anyway—or take an easier route. But without a guide, what then? Get advice before you leave. *By all means carry a map and use it.* Your outfitter will show you how to read and follow it, and he will advise you of the topography of the route.

Fine, but let's say the party is making a portage through rough country, and you're in the lead. You're on the trail one minute, the going easy. The next minute, suddenly and quite inexplicably, you and the rest of the party are off the beaten path and running smack into a swamp that shouldn't be there, heavy with evergreen and impossible to negotiate. One minute all was well, and now you don't know where you are or where the trail is, and you stop in bewilderment. At first you don't believe it, but as you search the surroundings, you run into nothing but that blank wall of foliage.

Watch it! This is the critical moment. Drop your pack and rest. Use your head instead of your feet. Your recent movements are still fresh in your mind. The trail can't be very far away. Sit down and try to relax. Now try to recall the last spot on which you were definitely on the trail. Retrace your route in your mind. Somewhere along the way you missed the path, or took the wrong one. Was it a few minutes ago? Was it longer than that?

Make this place your temporary camp. *Keep your party together.* Work out from here, blazing the trail as you travel, using your temporary camp as the hub of a wheel. Sight ahead for some prominent landmark and make a beeline for it. You should find your big lake shortly enough if you follow small streams to their outlet, and most portages between lakes parallel the streams that connect them.

Rely on your compass. Keep it tied to the breast pocket of your shirt and refer to it as you travel. If one track does not take you back to the right trail or to familiar water, try another, *working out from your temporary camp until you hit a place that rings a bell.*

Try to avoid all this in the first place, however, by

making a point of finding the right portage trail. Most portages are marked by a break in the shoreline vegetation, blazed trees, paint marks from canoes, old campfires, well-worn rocks. Don't head into overgrown country; if a trail hasn't been used, it is no portage.

Where the portage opening is hard to find, you may have to skirt the shore looking for it, paddling or poling through shallow water and heavy vegetation. But don't commit yourself to a trail until you're absolutely sure it is the right one.

Know where you are going at all times, and you'll enjoy the expedition so much more because of your confidence in being in command of the situation.

Separation

Never leave a party of walkers or canoeists to go off on your own. This is a general rule of outdoors activities. And if the rule is broken, certain precautions must be followed. First, if the party intends to split into small groups, each unit should be composed of at least two people. Second, if you intend to go off on your own, you should inform the others of your destination, route, and estimated time of return. Third, if you get separated from the others, *don't panic*. Shouts do not carry far, so carry a *whistle* at all times and use it for signaling. If the worse comes to the worst and you cannot contact the rest of the party, let them find you. They should begin an organized search as soon as they realize that you are missing.

19

Canoe Camping— Sources of Information

As you begin to plan your trip, it is important to know what you will face in the way of terrain, portages, climate, rivers, lakes, rapids, camps, outfitters, resorts, and other such things. It is also helpful and interesting to delve into the history and natural history of the area. In the United States you can write to the appropriate agency in the state you're planning to visit, explaining what you have in mind and the part of the state you expect to be in. The state recreation, park, or conservation department will then supply maps and information on that area. (See Appendix I for addresses of state agencies.)

Some of the canoeing areas are fairly remote; others readily accessible. There is much to explore and enjoy on streams that are probably not very far away from you. Easy-flowing streams through the countryside can reveal the beauties of nature to the curious and alert-minded and allow the canoeist to fish and journey as leisurely as he desires through fascinating rural areas, maybe taking him to an open lake or a wider river.

Another important source of material for planning and making the canoe trip is the United States Department of the Interior, Geological Survey, Washington, D.C. 20240. Available here are the "State Topographic Map Index," an informative booklet entitled "Topographic Maps," and a sheet showing topographic map symbols. These are sent free of charge on request.

The U.S. Geological Survey unit is a quadrangle bounded by parallels of latitude and meridians of longitude. Printed in three colors, topographic maps show cultural features, such as roads, railroads, cities and towns, in black; water features in blue; and the features of relief, such as hills, mountains, and valleys, in brown contour lines. Unfortunately, these maps are not always current and therefore often do not depict such recent developments as superhighways, etc.

Maps covering areas in the states west of the Mississippi River (including all of Louisiana and Minnesota) should be ordered directly from the Distribution Section, Geological Survey, Federal Center, Denver, Colorado 80225. Maps for areas east of the Mississippi River (including Puerto Rico and the Virgin Islands) should be ordered from the Distribution Section, Geological Survey, 1200 South Eads Street, Arlington, Virginia 22202. The price of a standard quadrangle map is fifty cents.

The Ozarks in Arkansas and Missouri offer exciting and action-packed canoe routes, with scenic points of interest and top fishing areas. Some states with canoeing waters and fine camping possibilities are Virginia, Kentucky, Florida, Texas, Indiana, Tennessee, Pennsylvania, New Jersey, New Hampshire, and New York.

When you are considering a canoe trip into the more remote regions of the United States, certain states stand out for their special possibilities. Among others, Michigan, Wisconsin, Maine, Minnesota, Idaho, Colorado, Oregon, Wyoming, Washington, Nevada, and California offer unspoiled canoe country. The northern states have much in common in their rivers and connecting lakes, their coniferous forests, and their wild stretches of rugged scenery. And in all the states the canoe routes are varied, generally well mapped, and thoroughly enjoyable.

Minnesota offers the opportunity not only of canoeing through the justly famous and wild Superior National Forest but also of heading into Canada's huge, picturesque Quetico Provincial Park. Both of these regions abound in fish and wildlife, are for the most part remote, and are being preserved as a wilderness domain.

The waters of the Superior National Forest and Canada's Quetico are clear and cold, rockbound in many spots, island-studded, rich with spruce and pine, teeming with wildlife, and they offer unlimited possibilities for the man who loves the out-of-doors. The canoe routes available there are almost without number, allowing the canoeist to head in almost any direction and spend any amount of time exploring and camping.

A look at the map showing the canoe routes of the Superior-Quetico reveals that this area is encompassed in the two million square miles of Precambrian or Laurentian Shield that encircles Hudson Bay and makes up more than half of Canada. The map of this region shows a horseshoe-shaped area, rock-embedded, paved with the blue of, for the most part, interconnected rivers and lakes, and navigable much of the way by canoe. The canoe trip may be long or short, difficult or easy, as the outdoorsman desires, and he can choose from an almost unlimited procession of river and lake waters that almost defy the imagination.

Canada, especially, is a canoe traveler's dream. Specific information about canoe trips in each province may be obtained by writing to the department in charge. Names and addresses of offices in the provinces appear in Appendix I.

The Alaskan Highway also has opened up regions for the canoe traveler, who can now put in his canoe from some point along this roadway and travel as he wishes, through deep, rapid-strewn wilderness or along well-behaved waterways that wind calmly and leisurely through meadow and lowland. Today, as much as yesterday, Alaska, a country of unlimited natural wonders, lures the prospector, the explorer, the adventurer.

Lake Superior, especially along its more isolated shore waters, offers fine adventure and exploration by canoe. This is not the remote country it used to be, by any means, but a lifetime of exploration is possible along its winding, rockbound, enchanting shoreline, rich with its many tributaries and with wildlife— timberwolf, coyote, whitetail deer, to name only a few.

Some of the most enthusiastic canoe campers are the Boy Scouts. They not only have planned and organized canoe trips but have established headquarters and camps from which to start and return. For instance, qualified Scouts who wish to canoe into the Superior-Quetico regions may make arrangements through the Boy Scouts of America, Region 10, 238 Minnesota Building, St. Paul, Minnesota 55101, with the trips starting from the Sommers Wilderness Canoe Base, Ely, Minnesota.

Most of these Scout canoe trips are supervised by camp counselors and are made through country rich in scenery and good for fishing, with food depots and campsites available at strategic points along the way. The Y.M.C.A. also has a boys' camp and canoe base near Boulder Junction, Wisconsin, from which canoe trips begin and end.

State and Province
Information Sources

Alabama: Bureau of Publicity & Information, 304 Dexter
Avenue, Montgomery 36104. Also, Department of Conservation, Administrative Building, Montgomery 36104

Alaska: Department of Economic Development, Alaska
Travel Division, Pouch E, Juneau 99801

Arizona: Arizona Development Board, 3443 N. Central
Avenue, Suite 310, Phoenix 85012

Arkansas: Arkansas Publicity & Parks Commission, Room
149, State Capitol, Little Rock 72201

California: Department of Parks & Recreation, Box 2390,
Sacramento 95811

Colorado: Department of Public Relations, State Capitol,
Denver 80203

Connecticut: State Park & Forest Commission, Hartford
06115. Also, Connecticut Development Commission,
State Office Building, Hartford 06115

Delaware: State Park Commission, 3300 Faulkland Road,
Wilmington 19808. Also, Delaware State Development,
Tourism Division, 45 The Green, Dover 19901

District of Columbia: National Capital Region, National
Park Service, 1100 Ohio Drive S.W., Washington 20242

Florida: Florida Board of Parks, LeRoy Collins Building,
Gaines Street at Adams, Tallahassee 32304

Georgia: Georgia Department of State Parks, 7 Hunter
Street S.W., Atlanta 30334

Hawaii: Hawaii Visitors Bureau, Suite 801, Waikiki Business Plaza, Honolulu 96815

Idaho: Department of Commerce & Development, Room
108, State Capitol Building, Boise 83707

Illinois: Department of Conservation, Division of Parks & Memorials, Room 102, State Office Building, Springfield 62706

Indiana: Department of Natural Resources, Division of State Parks, 616 State Office Building, Indianapolis 46209. Also, Indiana Department of Commerce, Indiana Tourist Division, Room 334, State House, Indianapolis 46204

Iowa: Public Relations, State Conservation Commission, East 7th & Court, Des Moines 50308

Kansas: Department of Economic Development, State Office Building, Topeka 66612

Kentucky: Travel Division, Department of Public Information, Capital Annex Building, Frankfort 40601

Louisiana: State Parks & Recreation Commission, Old State Capitol Building, Drawer 1111, Baton Rouge 70821

Maine: State Park & Recreation Commission, State House, Augusta 04330. Also, Department of Economic Development, State House, Augusta 04330

Maryland: Department of Forests & Parks, State Office Building, Annapolis 21404. Also, Tourist Division, Department of Economic Development, State Office Building, Annapolis 21401

Massachusetts: Department of Natural Resources (Camping), 100 Cambridge Street, Boston 02202. Also, Department of Commerce & Development, Bureau of Vacation Travel, 100 Cambridge Street, Government Center, Boston 02202

Michigan: Michigan Tourist Council, Stevens T. Mason Building, Lansing 48926

Minnesota: Division of State Parks, 320 Centennial Office Building, St. Paul 55101. Also, Vacation Information Center, 57 West 7th Street, St. Paul 55102

Mississippi: Mississippi Park System, 1104 Woolfolk Building, Jackson 39201

Missouri: Missouri State Park Board, Box 176, Jefferson City 65101. Also, Division of Commerce & Industrial Development, Travel Recreation Section, Jefferson Building, Jefferson City 65101

Montana: Advertising Department, Montana Highway Commission, Helena 59601

Nebraska: Nebraskaland, State Capitol, Lincoln 68509

Nevada: Nevada State Park System, Room 221, Nye Building, 201 S. Fall Street, Carson City 89701. Also, Department of Economic Development, Carson City 89701

New Hampshire: Division of Economic Development, State House Annex, Concord 03301

New Jersey: Department of Conservation & Economic Development, Bureau of Parks, Box 1889, Trenton 08625. Also, State Promotion Section, Box 1889, Trenton 08625

New Mexico: State Park & Recreation Commission, Box 1147, Santa Fe 87501. Also, State Tourist Division, 302 Galisteo, Santa Fe 87501

New York: Conservation Department, Division of Lands & Forests, Bureau of Forest Recreation, State Campus, Albany 12226. Also, Division of Parks, State Campus Site, Albany 12226, and New York State Department of Commerce, Travel Bureau, 112 State Street, Albany 12207

North Carolina: Travel & Promotion Division, Department of Conservation & Development, Raleigh 27602

North Dakota: State Travel Division, State Highway Department, Highway Building, Bismarck 58501

Ohio: Ohio Department of Natural Resources, Division of Parks & Recreation, 913 Ohio Departments Building, Columbus 43215. Also, Development Department, Information Central, Room 1007, Ohio Departments Building, Columbus 43215

Oklahoma: Oklahoma Industrial Development & Park Department, Tourist Information Division, 500 Will Rogers Memorial Building, Oklahoma City 73105

Oregon: Travel Information Division, State Highway Department, Salem 97310

Pennsylvania: Bureau of State Parks, Room 601, Feller Building, 301 Market Street, Harrisburg 17101. Also, Travel Development Bureau, Department of Commerce, 113 South Office Building, Harrisburg 17120

Rhode Island: Division of Parks & Recreation, 83 Park Street, Providence 02903. Also, Rhode Island Development Council, Tourist Promotion Division, Roger Williams Building, 49 Hayes Street, Providence 02908

South Carolina: Department of Parks, Recreation & Tourism, Box 1358, Columbia 29202

South Dakota: Publicity Division, Department of Highways, Pierre 57501

Tennessee: Division of Information & Tourist Promotion, Department of Conservation, 2611 West End Avenue, Nashville 37203

Texas: Parks & Wildlife Department, John H. Reagon Building, Austin 78701. Also, Texas Highway Department, Travel & Information Division, Austin 78701

Utah: Utah Travel Council, Council Hall, Capitol Hill, Salt Lake City 84114

Vermont: Department of Forests & Parks, Montpelier 05602. Also, Vermont Development Department, Montpelier 05602

Virginia: Division of Parks, Suite 501, Southern State Building, Richmond 23219. Also, Virginia Department of Conservation & Economic Development, 911 E. Broad Street, Richmond 23219

Virgin Islands: Virgin Islands National Park, Box 1707, Charlotte Amalie, St. Thomas 00801

Washington: Visitor Information Bureau, General Administration Building, Olympia 98501

West Virginia: Division of Parks & Recreation, Department of Natural Resources, State Office Building, Charleston 25305. Also, Department of Commerce, Planning & Research Division, 1703 Washington Street E., Charleston 25311

Wisconsin: Vacation & Travel Service, Conservation Department, Box 450, Madison 53701

Wyoming: Wyoming Travel Commission, 2320 Capitol Avenue, Cheyenne 82001

Canada

Canada: Canadian Government Travel Bureau, 150 Kent Street, Ottawa, Ontario. Also write here for information on Northwest Territories

Alberta: Alberta Government Travel Bureau, 331 Highways Building, Edmonton

British Columbia: British Columbia Government, Department of Travel Industry, Parliament Buildings, Victoria

Manitoba: Tourist Branch, Department of Tourism & Recreation, Room 408, Norquay Building, Winnipeg 1

New Brunswick: Travel Bureau, Box 1030, Fredericton

Newfoundland & Labrador: Newfoundland & Labrador Tourist Development Office, Confederation Building, St. John's, Newfoundland

Nova Scotia: Nova Scotia Travel Bureau, Department of Trade & Industry, Halifax

Ontario: Ontario Department of Tourism & Information, 185 Bloor Street East, Toronto 5

Prince Edward Island: Prince Edward Island Travel Bureau, Box 940, Charlottetown

Quebec: Department of Tourism, Fish & Game, 12 Ste. Anne Street, Quebec

Saskatchewan: Tourist Development Branch, Power Building, Regina

Yukon: Yukon Department of Travel & Publicity, Box 2703, Whitehorse

Canoeing
Organizations

THE AMERICAN CANOE ASSOCIATION. Office of the Secretary, 400 Eastern Street, New Haven, Connecticut 06513

THE AMERICAN WHITEWATER AFFILIATION. Harold Kiehm, Membership Chairman, 2019 Addison Street, Chicago, Illinois 60618

UNITED STATES CANOE ASSOCIATION. Charles Moore, 6338 Hoover Road, Indianapolis, Indiana 46260

THE SIERRA CLUB. Mills Building & Tower, Room 1050, San Francisco, California 94104

THE PRAIRIE CLUB CANOEISTS. 38 South Dearborn Street, Chicago, Illinois 60603

AMERICAN YOUTH HOSTELS. 20 West 17th Street, New York 10011

BOY SCOUTS OF AMERICA. National Council, New Brunswick, New Jersey 08903.

APPALACHIAN MOUNTAIN CLUB. 5 Joy Street, Boston, Massachusetts 02108